.QUILT GIVING.

19 Simple Quilt Patterns to Make and Give

DEBORAH FISHER

Fons&Porter
CINCINNATI, OHIO

CONTENTS

introduction
Joyful Giving, Stitch by Stitch

What is your superpower? Come on—we all have one. I am a maker. Not as exciting as being invisible or shooting laser beams from my eyes, but it's what I've got.

In 2003, after years as a fine art maker, I decided to use my superpower for good. It was time to start making things that people could use and that would make them happy. For me, that meant making quilts to give and share. I launched the Bright Hopes Collaborative Quilt Project with my mother; our mission is to give those without a permanent home a sense of place, with a beautiful quilt.

Creating a quilt is always a gift.

Creating a quilt is always a gift. It may be a gift to yourself—either the actual quilt or the time to do what you love. It may be a gift to someone you love or to someone you may not even know. Your mission may be to create a quilt for each one of your grandchildren, to provide quilts for a local charity, or even to finally make a quilt for your own bed after years of sleeping under that old ratty comforter. A birthday, a wedding, or a holiday quilt. A new home, a new couch, a new baby quilt. A sick friend, a favorite teacher, a just-because-I-love-you quilt. There is always a good reason to make a giving quilt.

MAXIMUM IMPACT, MINIMAL FUSS

The quilts in *Quilt Giving* are designed for maximum impact. They are bold, streamlined designs that are easy to cut and piece. Not quick. Simple. What's the rush? Here, there are no complicated lists of 25 different size pieces to cut, no 350 half-square triangles to piece. You can take your time to enjoy the process and still have a quilt before the next ice age. There are quilts here that will be your go-to "good grief, the baby shower/birthday/holiday is in two weeks!" gift. This does not mean slapdash sewing, bad craftsmanship, or low-quality materials! These projects are solidly doable, and the finished quilt will be even more beautiful because of it.

Making giving quilts is also the perfect opportunity to expand your sewing skills. Try something new. My designs in this book have a variety of compositional conventions. Map (page 60), Twinkle (page 80), Echo (page 92), and Bloom (page 104) take a block and go big for maximum impact. Summer (page 28), Sprinkle (page 42), and Gem (page 74) use easy corner triangles for a simple detail. City (page 24), Path (page 48), Forest (page 54), Bolt (page 98), and Garden (page 124) do away with traditional blocks and use a vertical or horizontal grid.

Make sure your sewing is giving back to you as well as to the recipient of your quilt. One of the joys of my job is the opportunity to work with so many wonderful volunteers and community groups, such as scout troops, 4-H groups, and adult day treatment programs. Circus (page 112), Picnic (page 118), and Nest (page 130) can be made by yourself, but are designed to be made with groups. You may have a local or online group or sewing bee that you would like to work with. If you don't, please find one! It is a gift to yourself to be connected with like-minded creative makers.

Sew with care. Give your sewing away. Make yourself happy. Make other people happy. Your superpower is sewing smiles.

—Deborah

Tools and Techniques

Between choosing fabrics, cutting, piecing, and quilting, it is easy to get overwhelmed with the technical side of making a quilt. A quilt is a big project, but it doesn't have to be a scary one. There are a few things you need to know how to do, but the most important thing is to enjoy the process. Be sure to take your time and complete each step with care. Good craftsmanship is something every maker should aspire to—your gift will be that much more beautiful.

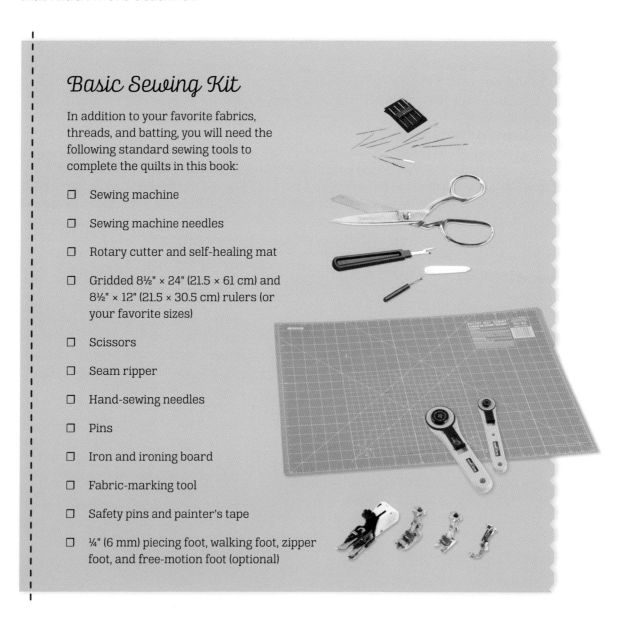

Basic Sewing Kit

In addition to your favorite fabrics, threads, and batting, you will need the following standard sewing tools to complete the quilts in this book:

☐ Sewing machine

☐ Sewing machine needles

☐ Rotary cutter and self-healing mat

☐ Gridded 8½" × 24" (21.5 × 61 cm) and 8½" × 12" (21.5 × 30.5 cm) rulers (or your favorite sizes)

☐ Scissors

☐ Seam ripper

☐ Hand-sewing needles

☐ Pins

☐ Iron and ironing board

☐ Fabric-marking tool

☐ Safety pins and painter's tape

☐ ¼" (6 mm) piecing foot, walking foot, zipper foot, and free-motion foot (optional)

TECHNIQUES FOR MAKING YOUR QUILT

To make these quilts, you need to use only basic sewing and quilting techniques. They are specifically designed with simplicity in mind, so you can concentrate on color and careful cutting and stitching, while still creating a wonderful gift. If you are a beginner, you will find these basic techniques essential to many of your future sewing and quilting projects.

Corner triangles

To make Summer (page 28), Sprinkle (page 42), Spark (page 68), Gem (page 74), Twinkle (page 80), Echo (page 92), Bloom (page 104), and Picnic (page 118), you need to know how to make corner triangles. They are versatile features, adding interest to your quilt with minimal fuss.

① Follow the project instructions to cut the larger block fabric and the smaller squares for the corner triangles.

② On each small square, mark a diagonal line on the wrong side of the fabric from one corner to the opposite corner (figure 1).

③ With right sides facing, place the smaller square on the block fabric on the appropriate corner. The marked line should not go into the corner but should touch the two adjacent sides (figure 2).

④ Sew along the marked line.

⑤ Trim the seam allowance in the corner to ¼" (6 mm) (figure 3). Finally, press the corner triangle open to complete the corner (figure 4).

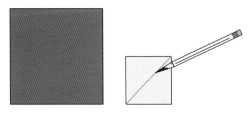

FIGURE 1

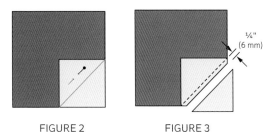

FIGURE 2   FIGURE 3

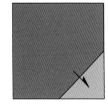

FIGURE 4

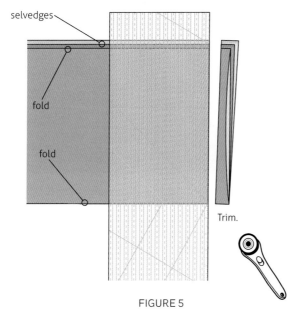

selvedges

fold

fold

Trim.

FIGURE 5

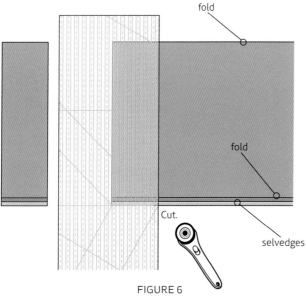

fold

fold

Cut.

selvedges

FIGURE 6

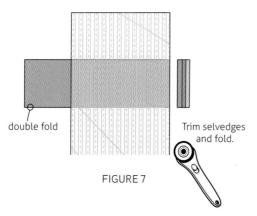

double fold

Trim selvedges and fold.

FIGURE 7

Cutting

The patterns in this book are designed for simple, efficient cutting. Be sure your rotary cutter is sharp and your mat and ruler are the proper size. For basic cutting of multiple shapes, such as squares—including those for corner triangles—and rectangles, fold the fabric in half, matching selvedges.

If the pieces you are cutting are small, you can fold the fabric in half again, matching the first fold to the selvedges. Trim the raw edges of the fabric square with the folded edges (**figure 5**). Then cut strips from the fabric (**figure 6**). Turn the strips 180° and cut off the selvedges and the fold (**figure 7**). Cut the strips into the required number of squares or rectangles (**figures 8 and 9**). If you are left-handed, you will need to follow the figures in mirror image.

Chain piecing

The same sections of a repeating pattern can be sewn more efficiently by chain piecing, rather than sewing them individually. To chain piece several of the same sections together, such as the rectangles and squares in Forest (page 54), match all of the pieces together, right side facing. Begin stitching one unit together. As you get to the end of the first unit, feed the next unit right behind it into the sewing machine (**figure 10**). Continue to feed in the units until all are sewn. Cut the threads between the units after you've finished sewing all of the sections.

Piecing quilt backs

Unless you use a very wide fabric or are making a very small quilt, you'll need to piece your quilt backing. Most of the quilts in this book will have two sections, with the seam running vertically.

To piece the back, cut the backing fabric in half widthwise so you have two equal pieces. Trim the selvedge edges off both sides of each piece. Place the two backing pieces right sides facing and sew down one long side.

Press the seam open. Trim and square up the backing if needed.

For large quilts, such as Bloom (page 104), you'll need to piece the backing in three sections. The seams will run horizontally.

Cut the backing fabric into three equal lengths. Trim the selvedge edges off both sides of each piece. Place two backing pieces right sides facing and sew down one long side. Add the third piece, right sides facing. Press the seams open. Trim and square up the backing if needed.

Making a quilt sandwich

After your top is complete, you will need to pin it to the batting and the backing, making a "quilt sandwich."

Press your top and your backing. Lay your backing right side down on the floor. Using masking tape or painter's tape, tape the backing to the floor. Work back and forth on opposite sides so the backing remains even and square. Lay the batting on top of the backing, smoothing it out from the center. Place the quilt top onto the batting right side up and smooth it out from the center. You can tape the top down also if you like. Starting from the center, pin the three layers together with safety pins, about 6" (15 cm) apart.

QUILTING

After you've sewn your quilt top and made a "quilt sandwich," you'll need to decide on how you would like to quilt it. You can quilt it with your machine, stitch it by hand, or tie it.

Using a sewing machine

With your sewing machine, you can either stitch free-motion or straight-line quilting. For most of the quilts in this book, I chose straight-line quilting designs to highlight the graphic nature of the piecing.

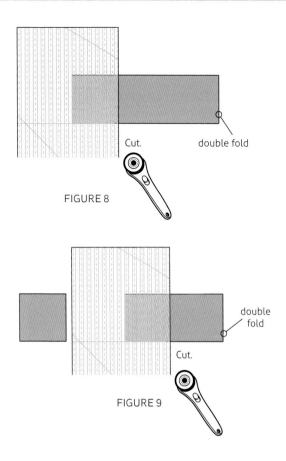

Cut.   double fold

FIGURE 8

double fold

Cut.

FIGURE 9

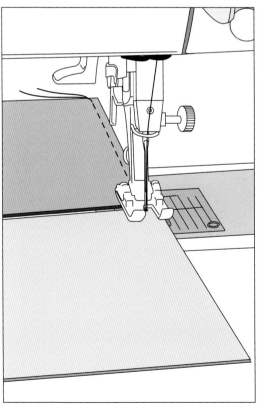

FIGURE 10

For straight-line quilting, use a walking foot on your sewing machine to evenly feed the quilt layers through the machine. You can create a variety of graphic designs from zigzags, as in Path (page 48), stripes, as in Echo (page 92), and grids, as in Circus (page 112). You can create a depth of textures by changing the direction and density of the lines, as in Map (page 60).

Hand quilting

Hand quilting, either big stitch or traditional, can add a wonderful variety of texture to your quilt. You can use it either by itself or in combination with other quilting techniques. Big stitch quilting uses thicker thread, pearl cotton, or floss, which in turn makes a bold stitch.

On Circus, I added some fun big-stitch hand quilting to the bright solid stripes. Use two or three strands of embroidery floss and sew a simple running stitch through a bunch of the stripes.

Tying

Tying is another way to add texture and color to your quilt and can be used exclusively in a quilt or with other techniques. Use embroidery floss to tie the three quilt layers together every few inches (or several centimeters) within the quilt. While a tied quilt is not quite as sturdy as a quilt with lots of machine stitching, tying is also simpler and quicker than other quilting techniques, and no less valid. Simply make double knots throughout your quilt to hold it together.

For Graph (page 20), the entire quilt is tied in every four-way corner. I used contrasting embroidery floss, but you can also use coordinating pearl cotton or any other strong yarn.

Take a stitch into the quilt and then back up again, making a stitch length of about $\frac{3}{16}$" (8 mm) on the back. Leave a tail of a few inches (or several centimeters). Knot the two ends together and trim to about $\frac{1}{2}$" (1.3 cm).

FIGURE 11

Long-arm quilting

You may want to send your quilt to a long-arm quilter, or if you have access to a long-arm quilting machine, quilt it yourself. Your local quilt shop may have a long-arm that can be rented by the hour or the day. While you can create beautiful and intricate designs, you can also use a long-arm machine to quickly stitch simple graphic lines. Many long-arm machines have a channel lock option that allows you to easily make lovely parallel lines.

Many of my quilts that were quilted with simple vertical or horizontal lines were done on a long-arm machine. This is a great way to become comfortable with the mechanics of using a long-arm machine before you jump into free-motion quilting.

Binding

The quilts in this book use 2½" (6.5 cm) wide strips for binding. Cut enough 2½" (6.5 cm) wide strips to generously go all the way around your quilt. Trim off the selvedge ends. Piece the short ends of the strips together to make one long binding strip. Press the seams open. Fold the entire binding in half lengthwise, wrong sides together, and press.

Trim the backing and batting even with your quilt top. Carefully match the raw edges of the binding to the raw edge of the front of the quilt. Starting about 6" (15 cm) from the beginning of the binding, use a ½" (1.3 cm) seam allowance to sew the binding to the quilt.

To make mitered corners, sew the binding to ½" (1.3 cm) from the adjacent side. Fold the strip of binding up at a 45° angle to the corner. Then fold the binding back toward the adjacent quilt side. Start sewing the next side ½" (1.3 cm) in from the corner **(figure 11)**.

Continue to sew the binding around the quilt until you get 12" (30.5 cm) away from where you first started attaching the binding. Overlap the binding and trim the end of the binding ½" (1.3 cm) past the beginning of the binding. Open both ends of the binding flat and piece them together with right sides facing. Finger press the seam open and refold the binding. Sew the joined binding section onto the quilt.

Fold the binding around to the back of the quilt and hand sew in place.

For a binding sewn entirely by machine, match the binding to the back of the quilt instead of to the front. After the binding is sewn, fold the binding around to the front of the quilt. Machine topstitch the binding in place. You can also zigzag the binding in place or use a decorative machine stitch.

For a decorative hand-stitched binding, match the binding to the back of the quilt. After the binding is sewn, fold the binding around to the front of the quilt. Using two or three strands of floss, stitch the binding in place with a running stitch.

LABELS

Every quilt needs some sort of label. If you are making only a few quilts, you can make your labels by hand. Or, you can have them printed or print them yourself. Be sure to leave enough space in your design if you are going to turn under the edges of the label.

Handmade label

To make your own labels, iron a piece of freezer paper to the back of a piece of fabric to stabilize it. Use fabric markers to draw or write your label information. Remove the freezer paper. Turn the edges of the label under and hand sew the label to the back of your quilt.

Printable fabric label

Sew-on printable fabric is a good option for a small batch of labels. Use whatever word-processing or graphics program you prefer on your computer. Make sure you have the printable fabric that is appropriate for your home printer. You may also want to make a test label to check the washability of your ink.

Printed labels

At Bright Hopes, we have several different label designs, which we have printed by Spoonflower, an online custom fabric-printing company. Our regular labels have our logo with a space to write the quilt recipient's name. We have a separate label that goes on all of our blankets that are given to newborns, as well as labels for partnership quilts and children's residence quilts.

I admit I am a bit obsessive about our labels. You probably don't need such an extensive collection, but you may want to have at least one to identify your work as an individual or as a group.

Sewing on a label

Our Bright Hopes labels come as yardage that we cut apart. We have incorporated a marked fold line printed on the label. We turn under the seam allowance to the fold line and hand sew around the label with a ladder stitch.

If you have a smaller label, you may want to sew it right into your binding as I do with my personal labels. Design the label to include seam allowances for the top and bottom. Fold the label in half lengthwise with right sides together and sew along the top and bottom. Then, turn the label right side out and sew the raw edge into the binding as you sew it.

Practical Matters
in Design

Whether you are sewing quilts for yourself, as gifts for loved ones, or even to donate to your favorite humanitarian organization, you must make some practical decisions. Depending on your focus, you may be sewing quilts for a variety of ages and genders. You may know the recipient very well, just a little, or maybe even not at all.

No matter who you're sewing for, here are a few tips to successfully design a quilt for anyone.

SIZE AND SHAPE

When designing quilts for children seven years old and up, I try to aim for about a 60" × 80" (152.5 × 203 cm) quilt. They almost never come out exactly this size due to block sizes and other design elements, but this is a good size for one small person.

For older boys and single adults, I try to go a bit bigger. For kids under seven, I go a bit smaller—a big quilt will swallow up a five year old. Smaller quilts are easier to wash, which the parents of toddlers will appreciate.

The shape of your quilt is just as important as the size of it. Square quilts can be lovely formats for design, but single beds are not squares, and people are not squares. (Well, not often.) For newborns, blankets are more practical than quilts. Blankets, pieced or whole cloth, are safer than even a small quilt when dealing with a tiny baby.

Try out Tender on page 34 or check out the Bright Hopes for Baby Blanket on page 152 in my book *Sew Fun: 20 Projects for the Whole Family.*

SITUATIONS AND SURROUNDINGS

Consider the circumstances of your recipient, whether it's your daughter, your father, your friend, or a child in need. How will the quilt enhance their surroundings, be a practical and beautiful object in their life, and give them comfort and joy?

A college student may have limited space in a dorm room and a narrow, extra-long bed. A grandparent may prefer a lap quilt to a bed-sized quilt.

MATERIALS

Consider your recipient, too, when choosing your materials. Does your niece live up north? What about an extra-cozy flannel backing? Way down south? How about a thin batting? If you are sewing for someone in a hospital, you may need to use specific materials. It is always best to ask before you spend money and time.

All that work and the cost of the materials really make any quilt an incredible gift. Everyone, no matter who your recipient is, deserves good-quality materials. Why do all that work with subpar materials? You will enjoy the process much more if you have wonderful materials, and the finished quilt will be that much more beautiful. Cotton quilting fabric is the most used material in quilting and is used for all the quilts in this book, but don't be afraid to try other materials. Consider wonderful linen and cotton/linen blends.

Fabric is expensive, so look for sales, save your scraps, piece your battings, try an alternate color scheme with the fabrics you have, but treat yourself and your recipient well.

COLOR AND PRINT

Working with fabric has its own practical color issues. Because we are not mixing our own colors, we are always on the hunt for "just the right yellow" or "that perfect shade of sky blue."

I am not a technical colorist, so I work with color intuitively. I use color so I can taste it. I combine colors so they sing to me.

Color may be primarily visual, but it seeps into your other senses. Why do I love chartreuse and lime green? Because they taste sour. Why do I put chocolate brown with hot pink and red with turquoise? Because alone they say one thing, but together they sing. But they may not sing to you. Put together colors that sing a song just for you. Use the colors that you can taste and smell. Now more than ever when we get constant visuals from blogs, websites, and social media, it is so important to be true to your own senses.

So what do you do when you are sewing quilts for others? Use what you are excited about but keep the recipients and their situations in mind. For me, that still means bold color!

Most of the quilts I design are for the Bright Hopes organization, which gives them to children and women in transitional housing. I rarely know my recipients, so I am guessing what they will like and hoping for the best. There is not much in the way of color in most shelter situations, so I like to bring vibrant, rich, joyful color to them.

I do not use much white or many very light colors in my designs. I believe that giving a quilt with lots of white negative space to an 8-year-old boy is totally impractical. At Bright Hopes, we are sometimes asked to avoid using large amounts of red because red is a gang color. I know. Gangs. Quilts. What? But there it is. But these are my quilt recipients. If you are making a quilt as a gift for someone who loves white (or gray or black or red), then choose the hues you know he'll love.

Aside from color, we sewists are also lucky enough to have many incredible prints to work with. But as with color, you need to use prints that fill your heart. I am a big fan of polka dots, as you can tell from the quilts in this book. You may love florals. What does your quilt recipient love? No matter what she likes, think twice about using subjective, character, or novelty prints unless you are using an assortment, such as in an I-Spy quilt. Favorite characters are fleeting, and you want your gift to have longevity.

Chapter 1
Simple Gifts

Simple quilts can be the most beautiful. Made by a beginning sewist, they instill confidence and success. They can be made by an experienced sewist who wants to enjoy the meditative nature of sewing without all the fuss. Simple quilts give you the flexibility and time to try something a little different than you might usually do with colors, solids, or prints.

These quilts are perfect to make when you need some sewing time to fill you up. Not quilt-math figuring, complicated cutting, tricky sewing time. Just lovely, satisfying sewing time. And, of course, even a simple quilt makes a spectacular gift.

In this chapter, you will find dynamic quilts made from just squares and rectangles and maybe bits of triangles for detail. You will also find a pieced and quilted baby blanket with a pocket and a softie. Any of these projects is sure to be received with joy. Go ahead—feel all powerful. You are sewing smiles.

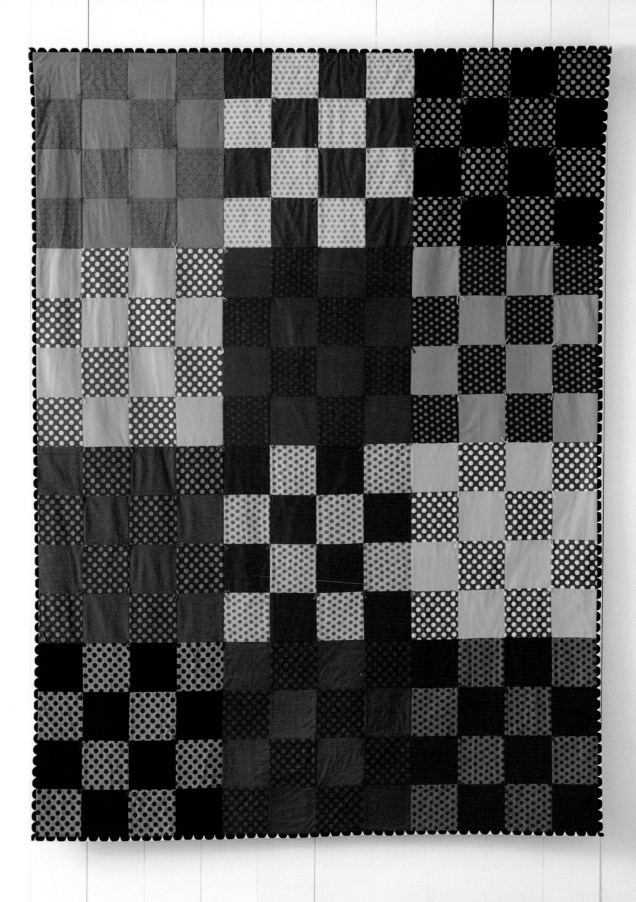

GRAPH

FINISHED SIZE
54" × 72" (137 × 183 cm)

MATERIALS
- ☐ 12 different polka dot fat quarters (or ¼ yd [23 cm] cuts fabric A)
- ☐ 12 different solid fat quarters (or ¼ yd [23 cm] cuts fabric B)
- ☐ 3½ yd (3.2 m) backing fabric
- ☐ ⅝ yd (57 cm) binding fabric
- ☐ 62" × 80" (157.5 × 203 cm) batting
- ☐ 5 skeins of coordinating embroidery floss

Note: Each block requires 1 fat quarter (or ¼ yd [23 cm]) of fabric A and 1 fat quarter (or ¼ yd [23 cm]) of fabric B. For the quilt shown here, each of the 12 blocks has a different solid and a different polka dot fabric, requiring 12 different fabric A pieces and 12 different fabric B pieces. If you plan to use fewer fabrics, multiply the ¼ yd (23 cm) needed by the number of blocks where you will use the fabric.

TOOLS
- ☐ Basic Sewing Kit (page 6)
- ☐ Embroidery needle

Super simple design makes this 16-patch quilt perfect for experimenting with bold color combinations. Here, I used my favorite polka dots paired with rich solids, but you could use all solids or all prints. Choose one contrasting pairing such as complementary colors, low-volume fabrics and darks, or black-and-white prints.

This simple gift is easy to personalize with the recipient's favorite colors and patterns. Try fussy-cut squares of some modern novelty prints for a fun I-Spy quilt.

For Graph, I decided that the simple squares and polka dot fabrics were perfect for a tied quilt. I used a different color floss for each block and tied the quilt at every four-way pieced corner.

CUT YOUR FABRIC

WOF = width of fabric

From each fabric A fat quarter:
- ☐ Cut 8 squares 5" × 5" (12.5 × 12.5 cm). Keep like colors together.

From each fabric B fat quarter:
- ☐ Cut 8 squares 5" × 5" (12.5 × 12.5 cm). Keep like colors together.

From binding fabric:
- ☐ Cut 7 strips 2½" (6.5 cm) × WOF. Trim the selvedges.

This quilt is also ideal for charm squares, pre-cut 5" × 5" (12.5 × 12.5 cm) pieces that are sometimes sold in individual color packets.

SEW THE BLOCKS

Note: All seam allowances are ¼" (6 mm).

① With right sides facing, for each block, sew four rows of four squares together, alternating fabric A and fabric B **(figure 1)**. Press seams toward the polka dot squares.

② Turn two of the rows 180°. With right sides facing, sew the four rows together into a large square, alternating the colors to create a checkerboard and aligning adjacent seams **(figure 2)**.

③ Repeat Steps 1 and 2 to sew each of the remaining 11 blocks.

ASSEMBLE THE TOP

④ With right sides facing, sew four rows of three blocks each. Make sure that fabric A from each block abuts fabric B from the adjacent block to continue the checkerboard pattern.

⑤ With right sides facing, assemble the quilt top by sewing the rows together in order as shown in the Graph Assembly Diagram.

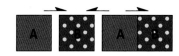

Make 4 rows for each block.

FIGURE 1

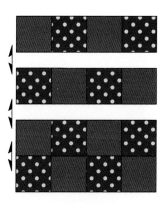

FIGURE 2

FINISH THE QUILT

⑥ Square the top. Pin it to the backing and the batting. Tie the quilt instead of machine quilting it. Add the binding. Turn to Tools and Techniques (page 6) for finishing techniques.

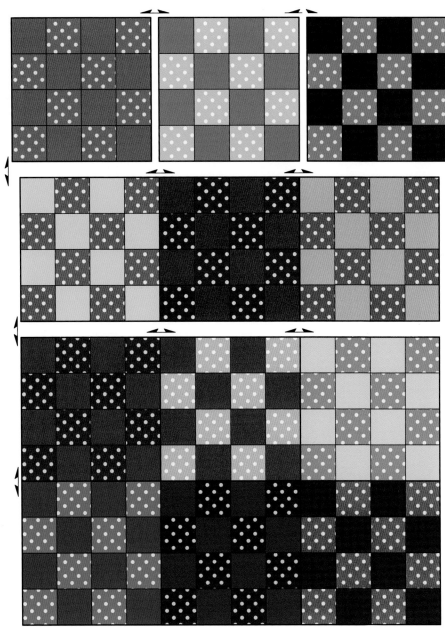

Graph Assembly Diagram

CITY

FINISHED SIZE
60" × 80" (152.5 × 203 cm)

MATERIALS
- ☐ 2½ yd (2.3 m) solid dark gray background fabric (A)
- ☐ ¼ yd (23 cm) grays, browns, blues, and coordinating low-volume prints each for 12 wide stripes (B)
- ☐ ¼ yd (23 cm) grays, browns, blues, lime green, and coordinating low-volume prints each for 6 narrow stripes (C)
- ☐ 5 yd (4.6 m) backing fabric
- ☐ ⅝ yd (57 cm) binding fabric
- ☐ 68" × 88" (173 × 223.5 cm) batting

TOOLS
- ☐ Basic Sewing Kit (page 6)

With an alternating arrangement, simple rectangles can create a dynamic quilt. Besides the main background fabric, there are eighteen vertical stripes—twelve wide and six narrow. I used nine different fabrics to create the striped rows. You can use as few as three fabrics (one for each of the two adjacent wide stripes and one for the narrow stripe) or as many as eighteen fabrics, a different one for each stripe. A variety of subtle colors allows you to highlight certain design elements simply, such as the center rows of lime green and the bright orange binding.

The City stripes are based on an 8½" (21.5 cm) measurement for easy cutting that is perfect for beginners. To cut the strips, fold the fabric selvedge-to-selvedge and then selvedge-to-folded-edge and cut four strips at once (page 6). You will have three extra strips, which you can use for fabric collages or scrap quilts, such as Picnic (page 118), Garden (page 124), or Nest (page 130).

CUT YOUR FABRIC

WOF = width of fabric

From fabric A:
- ☐ Cut 10 strips 8½" × 30½" (21.5 × 77.5 cm).

From fabrics B each:
- ☐ Cut 5 rectangles 4½" × 8½" (11.5 × 21.5 cm). *Note: If using the cutting technique noted on page 25, you will cut 8 strips, but you will use 5.*

From fabrics C each:
- ☐ Cut 5 strips 2½" × 8½" (6.5 × 21.5 cm). *Note: If using the cutting technique noted on page 25, you will cut 8 strips, but you will use 5.*

From binding fabric:
- ☐ Cut 7 strips 2½" (6.5 cm) × WOF. Trim the selvedges.

SEW THE BLOCKS

Note: All seam allowances are ¼" (6 mm).

① The stripes continue vertically through the entire length of the quilt, interrupted by the horizontal rectangles of background fabric. One set of stripes starts with a wide strip, and the other starts with a narrow strip. Keep track of the order of the strips as you piece them together.

Sew one narrow strip to the set of wide strips **(figure 1)**.

Repeat to make two more units in the same configuration using different colored stripes.

② With right sides facing, sew the three groups of strips together, creating a row of wide, wide, narrow; wide, wide, narrow; and wide, wide, narrow strips **(figure 2)**.

③ Make two different sets of five identical striped rows **(figure 3)** starting the second set with narrow, wide, wide strips.

ASSEMBLE THE TOP

④ With right sides facing and following the City Assembly Diagram, sew one set of five striped rows to five of the background fabric rows. Start with a background fabric and alternate the rows. Note the stripe color positioning.

⑤ Sew the remaining five striped rows to the remaining five background fabric rows. Start with a striped row and alternate the rows. Note the stripe color positioning.

⑥ With right sides facing, sew the rows together, making sure the stripes align vertically and matching adjacent seams.

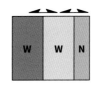

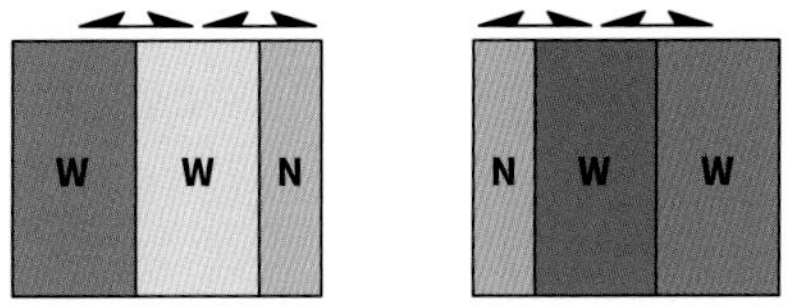

W = wide   N = narrow

FIGURE 1

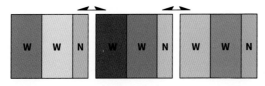

W = wide   N = narrow

FIGURE 2

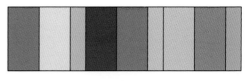

Make 5.

Make 5.

FIGURE 3

FINISH THE QUILT

⑦ Square the top, then pin it to the backing and the batting. Quilt as desired, then add the binding. I quilted City with horizontal and vertical lines to form a grid of random rectangles. Turn to Tools and Techniques (page 6) for finishing techniques.

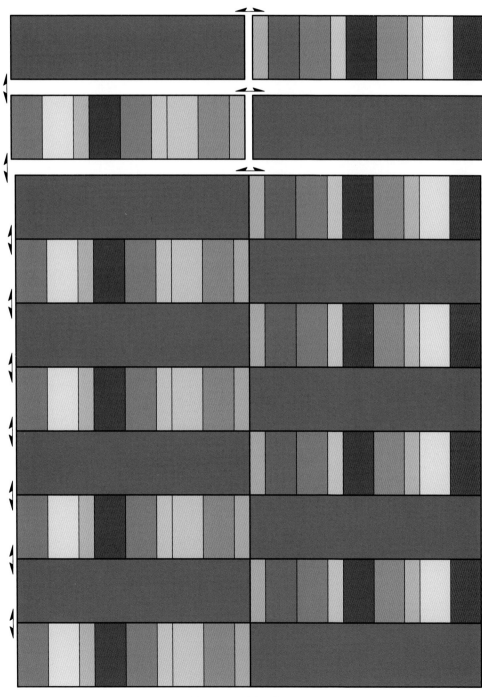

City Assembly Diagram

SUMMER

FINISHED SIZE
64" × 80" (162.5 × 203 cm)

MATERIALS
- ☐ 2½ yd (2.3 m) bright yellow solid fabrics (A)
- ☐ 2½ yd (2.3 m) hot pink solid fabrics (B)
- ☐ ¾ yd (68.5 cm) purple print fabrics (C)
- ☐ ¾ yd (68.5 cm) orange print fabrics (D)
- ☐ 4½ yd (4.2 m) backing fabric
- ☐ ⅝ yd (57 cm) binding fabric
- ☐ 72" × 88" (183 × 223.5 cm) batting
- ☐ Embroidery floss

TOOLS
- ☐ Basic Sewing Kit (page 6)

Summer is a versatile quilt that can be made as simple or as complex as you wish. The corner triangles add detail, so you can add as few or as many as you like or leave them off entirely. I used a variety of similar solid and print fabrics in two shades—bright yellow and hot pink—for the squares. Bold color choices will make even the simplest designs sing! The basic unit in Summer is a square with one corner triangle. Try turning blocks and moving them around within the grid to create a variety of different patterns.

To simplify the design, use just two similar fabrics for one set of squares and two similar fabrics for the other set, then alternate them within the rows. Whatever color palette you choose, you will need forty squares of each set of fabrics. Use scraps for the corner triangles or just two different fabrics. Summer is simple enough to sew with children to help them make a gift for a special person.

CUT YOUR FABRIC

WOF = width of fabric

From fabrics A and B each:
- [ ] Cut 40 squares 8½" × 8½" (21.5 × 21.5 cm).

From fabrics C and D each:
- [ ] Cut 40 squares 4½" × 4½" (11.5 × 11.5 cm).

From binding fabric:
- [ ] Cut 8 strips 2½" (6.5 cm) × WOF. Trim the selvedges.

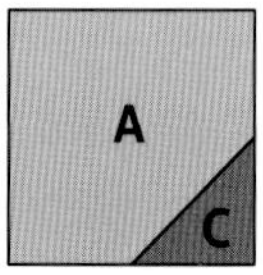

SEW THE BLOCKS

Note: All seam allowances are ¼" (6 mm).

① Pair each fabric A square with one fabric C square. With right sides facing, sew each fabric C square as a corner triangle (page 7) on one corner of a fabric A square (**figure 1**).

② Pair each fabric B square with a fabric D square. With right sides facing, sew each fabric D square as a corner triangle on one corner of a fabric B square (**figure 2**).

ASSEMBLE THE TOP

③ Make twenty rectangles with the A/C unit on the left and the B/D unit on the right. With right sides facing, sew one A/C block with the corner triangle in the upper left corner to one B/D block with the corner triangle in the upper right corner (**figure 3**).

④ Make twenty rectangles with the B/D unit on the left and the A/C unit on the right. With right sides facing, sew one A/C block with the corner triangle in the upper right corner to one B/D block with the corner triangle in the upper left corner (**figure 4**).

⑤ With right sides facing, sew the rectangles into blocks. Using one rectangle from Step 3

FIGURE 1

FIGURE 2

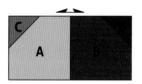
Make 20.

FIGURE 3

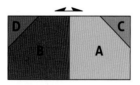
Make 20.

FIGURE 4

and one rectangle from Step 4 for each block, make ten blocks with the corner triangles pointing out **(figure 5)** and ten blocks with the corner triangles pointing in **(figure 6)**.

⑥ With right sides facing, sew five horizontal rows of four blocks each, alternating the two squares, starting with the corner triangles facing out on the right side of the row. Keeping the orientation, sew the rows together to complete the quilt top as shown in the Summer Assembly Diagram.

FINISH THE QUILT

⑦ Square the top, then pin it to the backing and the batting. Quilt as desired, then add the binding. I quilted Summer simply with horizontal, vertical, and diagonal lines. I also added ties of embroidery floss at the apex of each triangle. Turn to Tools and Techniques (page 6) for finishing techniques.

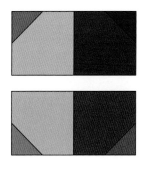
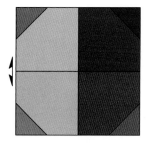

Make 10.

FIGURE 5

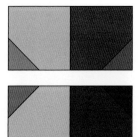
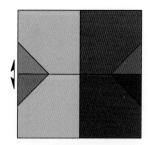

Make 10.

FIGURE 6

Summer Assembly Diagram

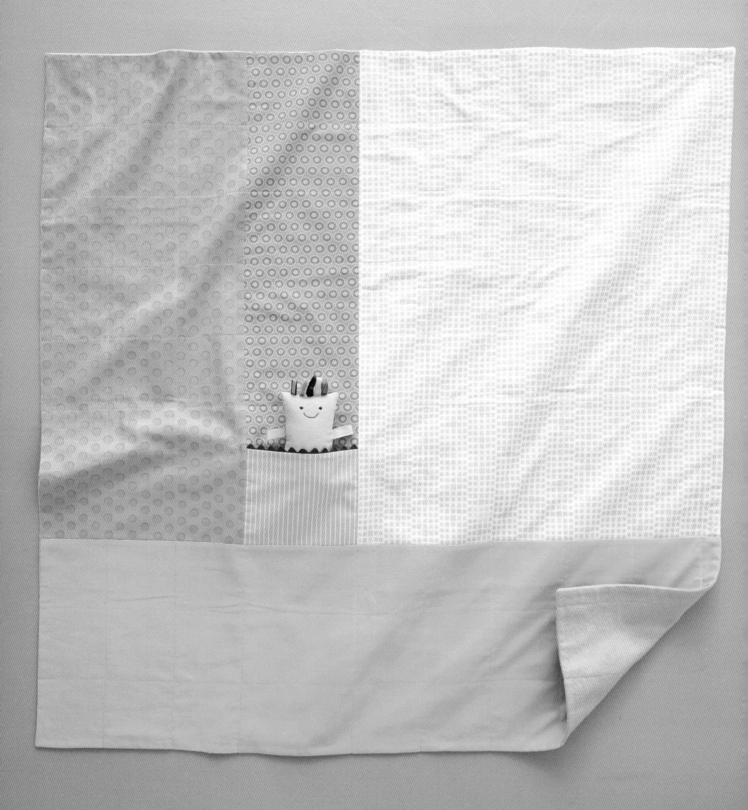

TENDER

FINISHED SIZE
30" × 30" (76 × 76 cm)

MATERIALS
- ☐ ⅛ yd (11.5 cm) or 1 fat quarter pale chartreuse stripe fabric (A)
- ☐ ¼ yd (23 cm) orange polka dot fabric (B)
- ☐ ⅜ yd (34.5 cm) gray-and-yellow polka dot fabric (C)
- ☐ ½ yd (45.5 cm) low-volume green polka dot fabric (D)
- ☐ ⅜ yd (34.5 cm) solid turquoise fabric (E)
- ☐ 1 yd (90 cm) flannel backing
- ☐ 6" (15 cm) coordinating medium rickrack (optional)

TOOLS
- ☐ Basic Sewing Kit (page 6)

Even crib-size quilts are too large and bulky for newborns. Tender is a lightweight quilted blanket pieced from quilting cottons coupled with a soft flannel backing. There is no batting, so the blanket is the perfect weight for tucking and swaddling a newborn.

This blanket is made extra special by the integrated pocket trimmed in rickrack. The pocket can hold a gift for a new mom or keep a pacifier handy, or you can pop in a simple-to-make Friend for a wonderful surprise.

CUT YOUR FABRIC

From fabric A:

☐ Cut 2 rectangles 4½" × 5½" (11.5 × 14 cm).

From fabric B:

☐ Cut 1 strip 5½" × 21½" (14 × 54.5 cm).

From fabric C:

☐ Cut 1 strip 9½" × 21½" (24 × 54.5 cm).

From fabric D:

☐ Cut 1 rectangle 16½" × 21½" (42 × 54.5 cm).

From fabric E:

☐ Cut 1 strip 9½" × 30½" (24 × 77.5 cm).

From flannel backing:

☐ Cut 1 square 30½" × 30½" (77.5 × 77.5 cm).

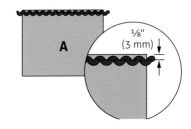

FIGURE 1

FIGURE 2   FIGURE 3

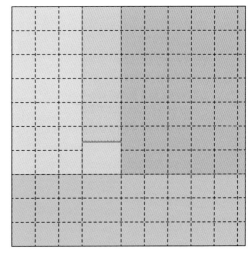

FIGURE 4

SEW THE TOP

Note: All seam allowances are ¼" (6 mm).

① Make the pocket. If you are using rickrack, lay it along the right side of one 5½" (14 cm) edge of one fabric A rectangle. Baste or sew it to the fabric using a ⅛" (3 mm) seam allowance (**figure 1**).

② With right sides facing, place the second fabric A rectangle on top of the first one. Sew the two rectangles together along the side with the rickrack (**figure 2**).

③ Turn the pocket right side out and press so the rickrack extends along the upper edge (**figure 3**).

④ Lay out the fabric B strip right side up. Place the pocket, right side up, on top of the strip, matching the bottom edges, as shown in the Tender Assembly Diagram. Pin the pocket in place, keeping the pins in the center of the pocket.

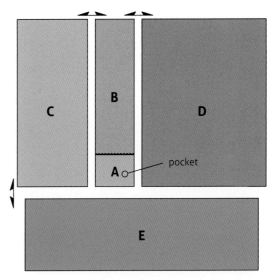

Tender Assembly Diagram

⑤ With right sides facing, sew the left long side of the A/B unit to a long side of the fabric C strip.

⑥ With right sides facing, sew the right long side of the A/B unit to a long side of the fabric D rectangle.

⑦ With right sides together, sew one long side of the fabric E strip to the bottom of the A/B/C/D unit.

⑧ Press the blanket top and trim to 30½" (77.5 cm) square if needed.

ASSEMBLE THE BLANKET

Note: If you would like to make a heavier weight blanket, use batting inside. Cut a piece of thin batting the same size as the flannel backing and use your hands to adhere the batting to the wrong side of the flannel. When layering the top and back with right sides together, make sure the batting is on the outside. Then, when you turn the blanket right side out after the sides are sewn, the batting will be sandwiched between the layers.

⑨ With right sides facing, sew the pieced top and flannel backing together on all four sides, leaving a 5" (12.5 cm) opening in the center of one side for turning.

⑩ Trim the seam allowance on each corner to reduce bulk. Turn the blanket right side out through the opening.

⑪ Carefully push out the corners and smooth all the seams from the inside. Press gently. Sew the opening closed by hand or machine.

FINISH THE BLANKET

⑫ Pin the blanket layers together to keep them from shifting during quilting. Quilt the blanket as desired, working around the pocket location.

Make Tender in a vibrant colorway with a matching bird Friend.

I stitched long straight lines along the sides and bottom of the pocket, extending beyond the pocket to the edges of the blanket. Then I stitched a grid of lines at 3" (7.5 cm) intervals **(figure 4)**.

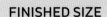

FRIEND

This simple softie is perfect to pop into Tender's pocket. With just a rectangle, ribbon scraps, and a few quick stitches for the face, you can create extra smiles. Use a leftover scrap from Tender to coordinate or use any other scraps you may have to suggest a cat, a bird, or a monster.

As always, when sewing for babies and young children: safety first. Make sure all seams are secure and ribbons are firmly sewn into the seam. Shortening your stitch length will help make seams stronger.

FINISHED SIZE
About 4" × 6" (10 × 15 cm), including appendages

MATERIALS
- ☐ 2 scrap fabrics, at least 3" × 5" (7.5 × 12.5 cm) each
- ☐ Handful of cotton, wool, or polyester stuffing
- ☐ 2 colors embroidery floss

For the cat:
- ☐ Four 2½" (6.5 cm) pieces of ⅜" to ½" (1 to 1.3 cm) wide ribbon
- ☐ Two 2" (5 cm) pieces of ¾" to 1" (2 to 2.5 cm) wide ribbon

For the bird:
- ☐ Nine 2½" (6.5 cm) pieces of ¼" to ⅜" (6 mm to 1 cm) wide ribbon

For the monster:
- ☐ Four 2½" (6.5 cm) pieces of ⅜" to ½" (1 to 1.3 cm) wide ribbon
- ☐ Five 2½" (6.5 cm) pieces of ¼" (6 mm) wide ribbon

TOOLS
- ☐ Basic Sewing Kit (page 6)
- ☐ Friend template (page 138)

CUT YOUR FABRIC

From the fabric scraps:

☐ Cut 2 rectangles 3" × 5" (7.5 × 12.5 cm) using the template on page 138.

SEW THE FRIEND

Note: All seam allowances are ¼" (6 mm).

① Following the diagrams on page 41, embroider the face for your friend, positioning the features about ¾" (2 cm) from the top of the rectangle.

Use a few tiny stitches for the eyes. Use a satin stitch for the cat's nose or the bird's beak. Use a double running stitch for the monster's mouth.

② For the cat, fold each 2" (5 cm) long piece of ribbon into an ear. Fold one ribbon in half widthwise to mark the center. Unfold the ribbon and fold the ends of the ribbon downward to create a point at the center top **(figure 1)**.

Fold each of the 2½" (6.5 cm) long ribbons in half widthwise to make legs. Following the placement markings on the template, pin the ribbons to the right side of the front. Match raw edges and point the ribbons toward the body. Stitch around the rectangle ⅛" (3 mm) from the edge, catching the ribbons **(figure 2)**.

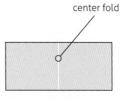

center fold

fold

FIGURE 1

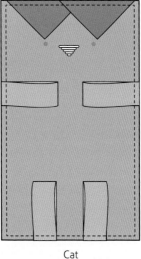

Cat

FIGURE 2

For the bird, fold the nine ribbons in half widthwise to make feathers and wings. Following the placement markings on the template, pin the ribbons to the right side of the front, matching raw edges and pointing the ribbons toward the body. Stitch around the rectangle ⅛" (3 mm) from the edge, catching the ribbons (figure 3).

For the monster, fold the nine ribbons in half widthwise. The wider ribbons will be the arms and legs, and the narrower ribbons will be the hair. Following the placement markings on the template, pin the ribbons to the right side of the front, matching raw edges and pointing the ribbons toward the body. Stitch around the rectangle ⅛" (3 mm) from the edge, catching the ribbons (figure 4).

ASSEMBLE THE FRIEND

③ With right sides facing, pin the second fabric rectangle to the front body. Sew around all four sides of the Friend, leaving the opening on the side as indicated on the template.

④ Trim the corners to eliminate bulk. Turn the Friend right side out through the small opening, carefully pushing out the corners and smoothing the seams from the inside.

⑤ Stuff the Friend. Hand stitch the opening closed.

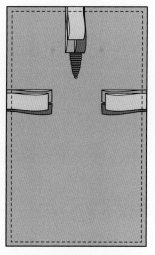

Bird

FIGURE 3

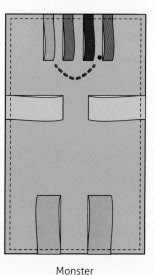

Monster

FIGURE 4

Embroidery Stitches for the Friends

To embroider the face on your Friend, use three strands of embroidery floss.

For the eyes, make several small stitches next to each other (figure 1).

For the Cat nose and Bird beak, use a satin stitch to fill in the triangle shape. Starting at the upper left corner of the nose or beak, bring the needle up through the fabric and then down again at the upper right corner (figure 2). You will have a long stitch on top of the fabric. Bring the needle back up just next to where you first came up and then down again where you first went down. Make this stitch slightly smaller than the first one because you are angling the triangle. Continue in this manner until you have filled in the nose or beak.

For the Monster mouth, make a row of small running stitches along the curve of the mouth (figure 3). Reverse the direction of your stitches and make running stitches along the same curved line, filling in the spaces made by the first row of stitches.

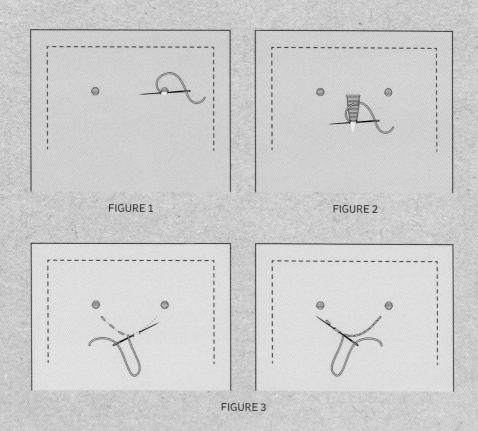

FIGURE 1

FIGURE 2

FIGURE 3

SPRINKLE

FINISHED SIZE
48" × 66" (122 × 168 cm)

MATERIALS
- ☐ 3 yd (2.75 m) solid salmon background fabric (A)
- ☐ ¾ yd (68.5 cm) print fabric (B) or 72 fabric scraps, each measuring at least 3½" × 3½" (9 × 9 cm)
- ☐ 3¼ yd (3 m) backing fabric
- ☐ ½ yd (45.5 cm) binding fabric
- ☐ 56" × 74" (142 × 188 cm) batting

TOOLS
- ☐ Basic Sewing Kit (page 6)

Sprinkle is perfect for using scraps of wonderful fabrics and also for trying out some new color possibilities in the negative space. White or gray may be safe go-to colors for the background, but a tint of a color will add depth. Here, the salmon pink shot cotton background enriches the entire quilt while highlighting the print scraps.

The design is simple, using only corner triangles for detail. Sewn together, the triangles create hourglass shapes. The use of both full and half-size rectangular blocks creates the brick repeat pattern. The key to matching the points at the center of each hourglass is pressing the seams. On one side of the hourglass, press the seam toward the corner triangles. On the other side, press the seam away from the corner triangle. The seams will interlock when you sew the short ends of the rectangles together to make the rows.

CUT YOUR FABRIC

WOF = width of fabric

From fabric A:

☐ Cut 16 strips 6½" × 24½" (16.5 × 62 cm).

☐ Cut 12 rectangles 6½" × 12½" (16.5 × 31.5 cm).

From fabric B or various scraps:

☐ Cut 72 squares 3½" × 3½" (9 × 9 cm).

From binding fabric:

☐ Cut 6 strips 2½" (6.5 cm) × WOF. Trim the selvedges.

SEW THE BLOCKS

Note: All seam allowances are ¼" (6 mm).

① Make sixteen full blocks. With right sides facing, sew a fabric B square as a corner triangle (page 7) onto each corner of the 6½" × 24½" (16.5 × 62 cm) fabric A rectangles (**figure 1**).

② Make twelve half blocks. With right sides facing, sew a fabric B square as a corner triangle onto two corners of each 6½" × 12½" (16.5 × 31.5 cm) fabric A rectangle. Make sure the two corners are on the same short end of the rectangle (**figure 2**).

ASSEMBLE THE TOP

③ Make six A rows. With right sides facing, sew one half block to each end of one full block, matching the short ends with the corner triangles (**figure 3**).

④ Make five B rows. With right sides facing, sew two full blocks together, matching the short ends with the corner triangles (**figure 4**).

⑤ Assemble the quilt top by sewing the rows together in order. With right sides facing, alternate A and B rows, beginning and ending with an A row as shown in the Sprinkle Assembly Diagram.

FINISH THE QUILT

⑥ Square the quilt top, then pin it to the backing and the batting. Quilt as desired, then add the binding. I quilted Sprinkle in a combination of echo quilting and horizontal lines. Turn to Tools and Techniques (page 6) for finishing techniques.

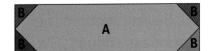

Full block
Make 16.

FIGURE 1

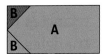

Half block
Make 12.

FIGURE 2

Row A
Make 6.

FIGURE 3

Row B
Make 5.

FIGURE 4

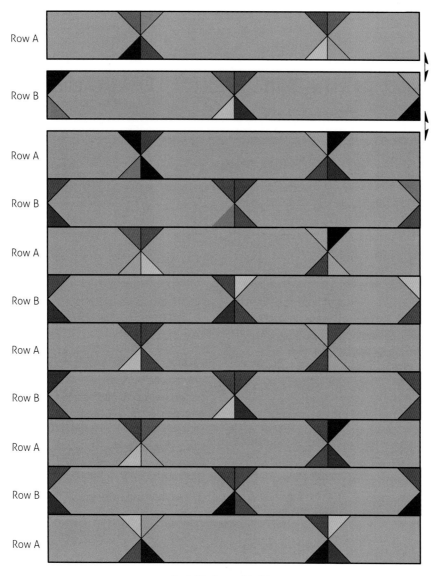

Row A

Row B

Row A

Row B

Row A

Row B

Row A

Row B

Row A

Row B

Row A

Sprinkle Assembly Diagram

A Project for the Kids: Fabric Collages

We, as makers and sewists, have materials. We have scraps, bits of ribbon, buttons, whatever. We have the stuff of making. And in turn, our children, grandchildren, and their friends are exposed to those materials for making. I am always amazed to be reminded that many people are not. They do not walk around with thread stuck to their shirt. They are not daily, weekly, or even monthly makers. It is our job to expose them to those materials. Remember that superpower?

To get kids started, encourage them to make a fabric collage. Fabric collages are a great project for all ages and can be made by an individual or a large group. You can work one-on-one with your favorite kid or create a mural at a party.

When my daughter was in her last year of preschool, it was my job one month to do something special with her class. Huge bags of scraps in my studio turned into a wonderful fabric collage! The colors, prints, and patterns had the preschoolers entranced. The theme that month was

buildings, so we made a huge cityscape collage that hung in the classroom for the rest of the year.

How you structure your collage time will depend on your situation, location, and participants. To introduce kids to quilting, you may want to have a quilt theme and make quilt-block collages. Or leave the project open to the imagination of the participants. Whatever you decide, don't forget to join in the fun. You may come up with a new quilt design in the process!

You don't need much, just:

☐ Fabric scraps pressed and cut into geometric shapes

Squares, rectangles, and triangles are all that you need, but you could cut your fabric scraps into other shapes as well. If you have a fabric die cutter you can make multiples very quickly. I like to have all of the fabric already cut for use and do not supply any scissors. This encourages creativity in using what is available. It also reduces frustration in trying to cut fabric with scissors and little hands.

☐ Glue, such as white school glue, brushes, and bowls

The natural impulse seems to be to put the glue on the fabric, but this creates a gluey ball of fabric and ruins the enthusiasm for the project. Instead, brush the glue onto the paper so the kids can apply the fabric on top.

☐ Paper for the collage background, such as sturdy roll paper for murals and smaller paper for individual collages

The only skills you need are the ability to cut fabric scraps, add paste to the background paper, and let the kids get messy.

PATH

FINISHED SIZE
54" × 68" (137 × 173 cm)

MATERIALS
- ☐ 1⅝ yd (149 cm) solid brown fabric (A)
- ☐ 2 yd (1.8 m) pale blue polka dot fabric (B)
- ☐ ⅜ yd (34.5 cm) solid orange fabric (C)
- ☐ 3½ yd (3.2 m) backing fabric
- ☐ ⅝ yd (57 cm) binding fabric
- ☐ 62" × 76" (157.5 × 193 cm) batting

TOOLS
- ☐ Basic Sewing Kit (page 6)

Path is a minimal quilt with great potential for showing off geometric quilting. I used a simple double chevron to echo the zigzag rows. You could highlight a wonderful large print or fussy-cut the center on-point squares. Whatever you choose, a striking combination of contrasting colors will give this minimal quilt high impact.

If you are new to triangles, there is no need to worry! Take your time with the triangle rows and the rest of the quilt top will go smoothly. The triangles in Path require care to keep the rows straight. They are cut as quarter-square triangles, so make sure the fabric's straight grain remains on the outer edge of the rows to prevent stretching.

CUT YOUR FABRIC

WOF = width of fabric ; LOF = length of fabric

From fabric A:

- [ ] Cut 2 LOF strips 8" × 54½" (20.5 × 138.5 cm).

- [ ] Cut 5 squares 7¼" × 7¼" (18.5 × 18.5 cm).

    - ▷ Cut the squares in half twice diagonally, from corner to corner. *Note: You will have 20 triangles, but will use just 18 of them. Save the leftovers for scrap quilts.*

From fabric B:

- [ ] Cut 2 LOF strips 20½" × 54½" (52 × 138.5 cm).

- [ ] Cut 9 squares 7¼" × 7¼" (18.5 × 18.5 cm).

    - ▷ Cut the squares in half twice diagonally, from corner to corner. *Note: You will have 36 triangles, but will use just 34 of them.*

    - ▷ Using the 2 extra triangles, cut them in half from the center of the longest side to the opposite corner to make 4 small triangles.

From fabric C:

- [ ] Cut 9 squares 4¾" × 4¾" (12 × 12 cm).

    - ▷ Cut 1 square in half once diagonally.

From binding fabric:

- [ ] Cut 7 strips 2½" (6.5 cm) × WOF. Trim the selvedges.

SEW THE QUILT TOP

Note: All seam allowances are ¼" (6 mm).

① Sew the eight rows of squares and triangles. With right sides facing, sew one fabric B triangle to the opposite sides of each fabric C square (**figure 1**).

② Sew one fabric B triangle to each of the two fabric C triangles (**figure 2**).

③ With right sides facing, sew the square and triangle units together to form one row for the quilt center (**figure 3**).

④ Sew the two remaining rows of triangles. With right sides facing, sew each of the 16 fabric A triangles to a large fabric B triangle (**figure 4**).

⑤ With right sides facing, sew each of the last two fabric A triangles to a small fabric B triangle (**figure 5**).

⑥ With right sides facing, sew half of the units together to form a row—eight units with a large A triangle/large B triangle

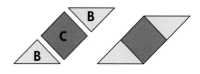

Make 8.

FIGURE 1

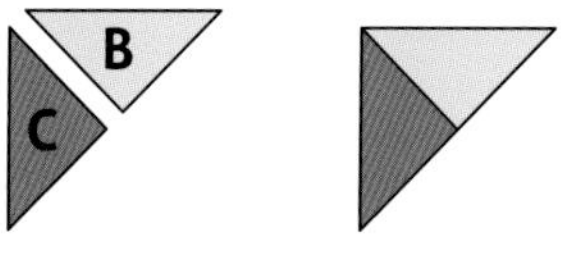

Make 2.

FIGURE 2

FIGURE 3

Make 16.

FIGURE 4

Make 2.

FIGURE 5

Make 2.

FIGURE 6

Path Assembly Diagram

and one unit with a large A triangle/small B triangle—and then add a small fabric B triangle to the opposite end to complete the row (**figure 6,** page 51).

Repeat to sew the remaining units and smaller fabric B triangles together to form another row.

ASSEMBLE THE TOP

⑦ Sew one 20½" × 54½" (52 × 138.5 cm) fabric B rectangle to each side of the center row of triangles as shown in the Path Assembly Diagram on page 51. Add the A/B pieced triangle rows on either side of the top, noting the color placement.

⑧ Sew one 8" × 54½" (20.5 × 138.5 cm) fabric A rectangle to the top and another on the bottom.

FINISH THE QUILT

⑨ Square the quilt top, then pin it to the backing and the batting. Quilt as desired, then add the binding. I quilted Path with lots of zigzags. Turn to Tools and Techniques (page 6) for finishing techniques.

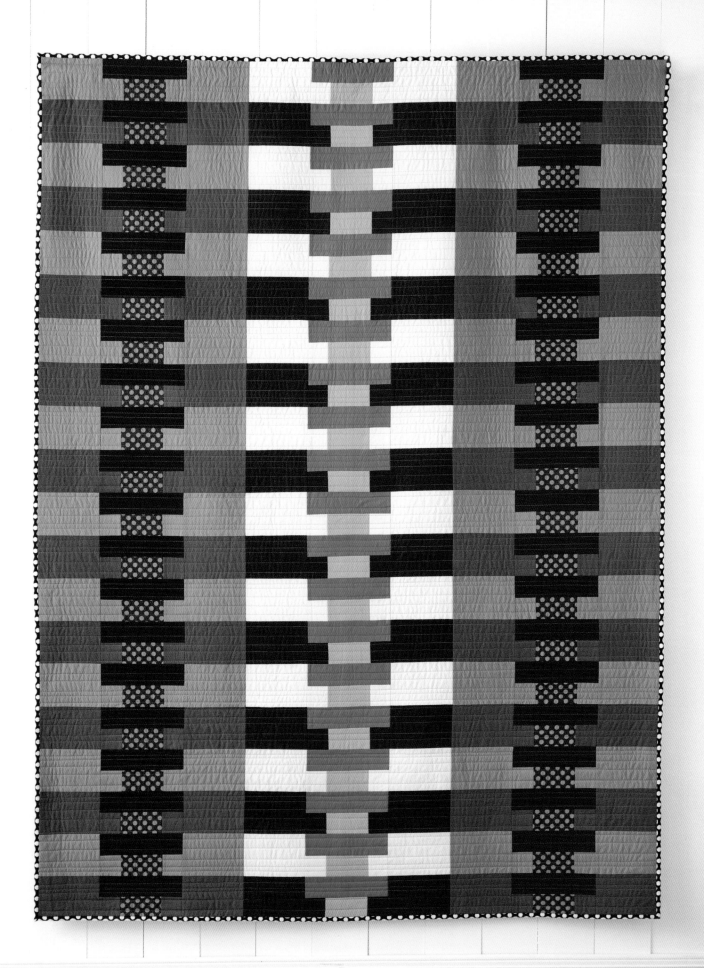

FOREST

FINISHED SIZE
60" × 80" (152.5 × 203 cm)

MATERIALS
- ☐ ½ yd (45.5 cm) solid turquoise fabric (A)
- ☐ ⅓ yd (30.5 cm) solid chartreuse fabric (B)
- ☐ ¾ yd (68.5cm) white fabric (C)
- ☐ ¾ yd (68.5 cm) solid dark brown fabric (D)
- ☐ ¾ yd (68.5 cm) solid dark red fabric (E)
- ☐ ½ yd (45.5 cm) turquoise polka dot fabric (F)
- ☐ 1¼ yd (114.5 cm) solid dark olive fabric (G)
- ☐ 1¼ yd (114.5 cm) solid grass green fabric (H)
- ☐ 5 yd (4.6 m) backing fabric
- ☐ ⅔ yd (61 cm) binding fabric
- ☐ 68" × 88" (173 × 223.5 cm) batting

TOOLS
- ☐ Basic Sewing Kit (page 6)

Forest is a great example of what you can do with just rectangles and squares, making for a simple gift with a sophisticated look.

Traditionally, we think of quilt blocks as squares arranged in rows, but in Forest, they take the shape of rectangles arranged in a vertical grid. Here, eight different fabrics are used to bring definition to the rectangular blocks. You can also simplify the design and use just four or six fabrics. The simple squares and rectangles of this quilt are perfect for chain piecing (page 8).

CUT YOUR FABRIC

WOF = width of fabric

From fabric A:
- ☐ Cut 20 rectangles 2½" × 8½" (6.5 × 21.5 cm).

From fabric B:
- ☐ Cut 20 rectangles 2½" × 4½" (6.5 × 11.5 cm).

From fabrics C and D each:
- ☐ Cut 20 rectangles 4½" × 6½" (11.5 × 16.5 cm).
- ☐ Cut 20 squares 2½" × 2½" (6.5 × 6.5 cm).

From fabric E:
- ☐ Cut 40 rectangles 2½" × 8½" (6.5 × 21.5 cm).

From fabric F:
- ☐ Cut 40 rectangles 2½" × 4½" (6.5 × 11.5 cm).

From fabrics G and H each:
- ☐ Cut 40 rectangles 4½" × 6½" (11.5 × 16.5 cm).
- ☐ Cut 40 squares 2½" × 2½" (6.5 × 6.5 cm).

From binding fabric:
- ☐ Cut 8 strips 2½" (6.5 cm) × WOF. Trim the selvedges.

SEW THE QUILT TOP

Note: All seam allowances are ¼" (6 mm).

① Sew the rectangular blocks together. You need sixty blocks total—twenty in each vertical row.

With right sides facing, sew a fabric C square onto each end of one fabric B rectangle. Matching the long sides, sew one fabric A rectangle onto the C/B unit. Sew one fabric C rectangle onto each end of the A/B/C unit (**figure 1**). Make ten of these units.

② With right sides facing, sew a fabric D square onto each end of the remaining ten fabric B rectangles. Matching the long sides, sew one fabric A rectangle onto the D/B units. Sew one fabric D rectangle onto each end of the A/B/D unit (**figure 2**). Make ten of these units.

③ With right sides facing, sew a fabric G square onto each end of one fabric F rectangle. Matching the long sides, sew one fabric E rectangle onto the G/F unit. Sew one fabric G rectangle onto each end of the E/F/G unit (**figure 3**). Make twenty of these units.

④ With right sides facing, sew a fabric H square onto each end of the remaining twenty fabric F rectangles. Matching the long sides, sew one fabric E rectangle onto the H/F unit. Sew one fabric H rectangle onto each end of the E/F/H unit (**figure 4**). Make twenty of these units.

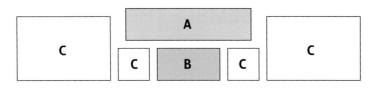

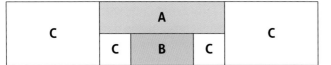

A/B/C unit
Make 10.

FIGURE 1

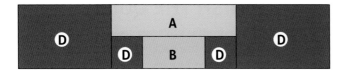

A/B/D unit
Make 10.

FIGURE 2

E/F/G unit
Make 20.

FIGURE 3

E/F/H unit
Make 20.

FIGURE 4

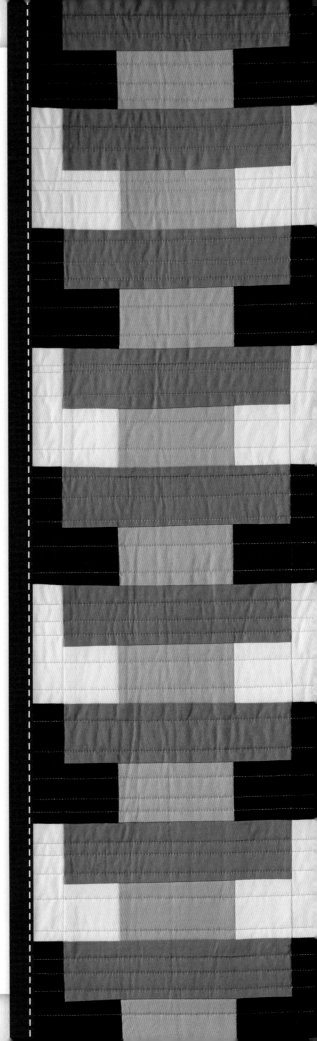

ASSEMBLE THE TOP

⑤ With right sides together, sew the blocks into three vertical columns. Sew the E/F/H units and the E/F/G units together in two columns of twenty blocks each, alternating the units and matching the long sides.

⑥ Sew the A/B/C units and the A/B/D units together in one column of twenty blocks each, alternating the units and matching the long sides.

⑦ Sew the three columns together as shown in the Forest Assembly Diagram, matching adjacent seams.

FINISH THE QUILT

⑧ Square the quilt top, then pin it to the batting and the backing. Quilt as desired, then add the binding. I quilted Forest with simple horizontal lines, randomly spaced. Turn to Tools and Techniques (page 6) for finishing techniques.

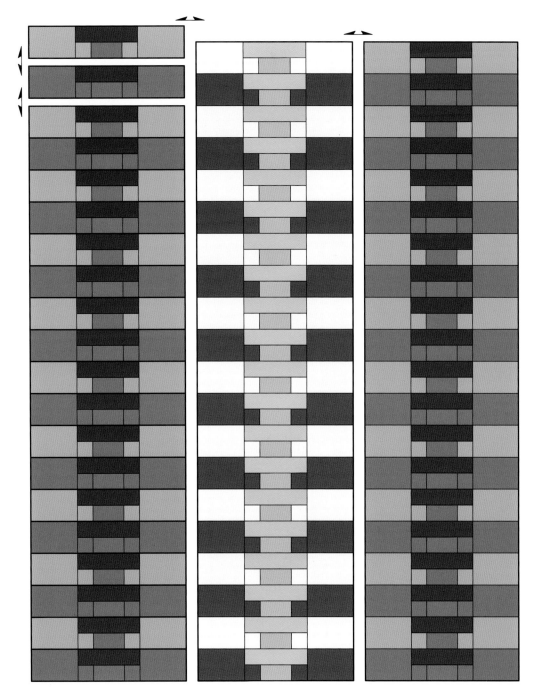

Forest Assembly Diagram

MAP

FINISHED SIZE
48" × 60" (122 × 152.5 cm)

MATERIALS
- ☐ 1¼ yd (114.5 cm) solid gray fabric (A)
- ☐ 1¼ yd (114.5 cm) solid wine red fabric (B)
- ☐ ⅜ yd (34.5 cm) solid and print hot pink fabrics (C)
- ☐ ¼ yd (23 cm) or 1 fat quarter solid pale pink fabric (D)
- ☐ ¼ yd (23 cm) or 1 fat quarter solid brown fabric (E)
- ☐ 3¼ yd (3 m) backing fabric
- ☐ ½ yd (45.5 cm) binding fabric
- ☐ 56" × 68" (142 × 173 cm) batting

TOOLS
- ☐ Basic Sewing Kit (page 6)

Map is a perfect-size quilt to make for a young child, and it's simple to construct. It's also great practice for piecing half-square triangles. I used a variety of coordinating red and pink fabrics for the contrasting triangles, but you could use just one fabric. Be sure to try some bold color combinations to highlight the triangles!

There are many ways to construct half-square triangles. I pair two squares and then mark them diagonally. I stitch two lines, one on either side of the marked line, and then cut the square on the marked line to make two triangle blocks at once.

CUT YOUR FABRIC

WOF = width of fabric

From fabrics A and B each:
☐ Cut 2 rectangles 12½" × 24½" (31.5 × 62 cm).

☐ Cut 2 rectangles 9½" × 18½" (24 × 47 cm).

☐ Cut 2 rectangles 10½" × 12½" (26.5 × 31.5 cm).

☐ Cut 2 rectangles 5½" × 8½" (14 × 21.5 cm).

☐ Cut 2 squares 3½" × 3½" (9 × 9 cm).

☐ Cut 9 squares 4" × 4" (10 × 10 cm).

From fabric C:
☐ Cut 18 squares 4" × 4" (10 × 10 cm).

From fabrics D and E each:
☐ Cut 2 rectangles 4½" × 5½" (11.5 × 14 cm).

From binding fabric:
☐ Cut 6 strips 2½" (6.5 cm) × WOF. Trim the selvedges.

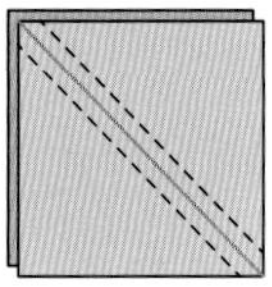

SEW THE BLOCKS

Note: All seam allowances are ¼" (6 mm).

Whatever method you use to make half-square triangles (HSTs), make sure they finish at 3½" (9 cm) square.

① Sew the HSTs. With right sides facing, make nine sets with the 4" × 4" (10 × 10 cm) fabric A squares and the remaining 4" × 4" (10 × 10 cm) fabric C squares.

Make nine more sets with the 4" × 4" (10 × 10 cm) fabric B squares and the 4" × 4" (10 × 10 cm) fabric C squares.

② Mark a diagonal line across each paired set from corner to corner. Sew a seam on each side of the marked line, ¼" (6 mm) away from the marked line (**figure 1**).

③ Cut each sewn square in half diagonally on the marked line (**figure 2**).

Press each square open and trim to 3½" × 3½" (9 × 9 cm) (**figure 3**).

④ Map is a double mirror image, so lay the pieces out first to make assembly simpler. Make each quarter of the quilt separately.

Make the two A/C/B/D quarters. Following the Map Assembly Diagram, lay out the half-square triangle blocks into two rows of four A/C blocks and two rows of five A/C blocks. With right sides facing, sew the squares into rows.

⑤ With right sides facing, sew one 3½" (9 cm) fabric A square to one end of each of the two rows with five A/C blocks.

⑥ With right sides facing, sew each of the two 4½" × 5½" (11.5 × 14 cm) fabric D rectangles to a 5½" × 8½" (14 × 21.5 cm) fabric B rectangle. Sew a 10½" × 12½" (26.5 × 31.5 cm) fabric B rectangle to each pieced rectangle. Add the A/C triangle rows, sewing the strip of four HSTs first and then the strip of five HSTs with the square. Add a 9½" × 18½" (24 × 47 cm) fabric A rectangle and

FIGURE 1

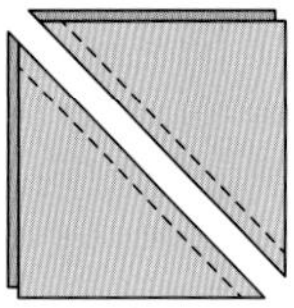

FIGURE 2

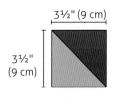

3½" (9 cm)

3½" (9 cm)

FIGURE 3

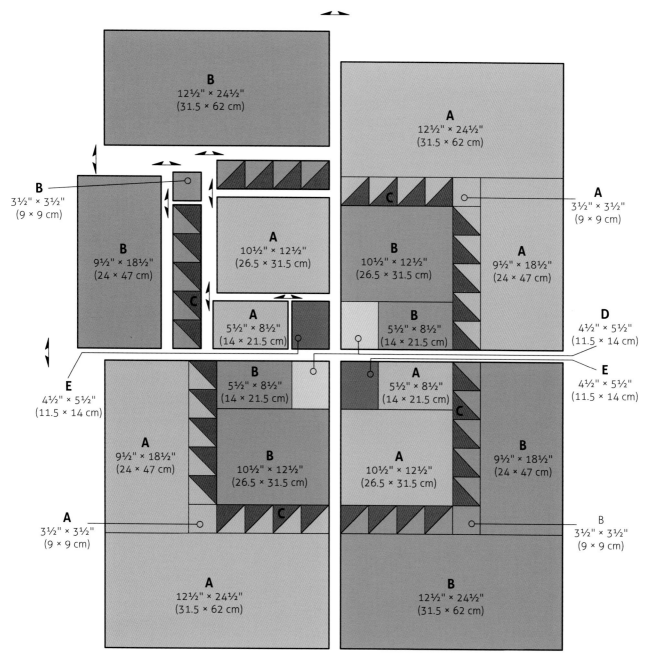

B
12½" × 24½"
(31.5 × 62 cm)

A
12½" × 24½"
(31.5 × 62 cm)

B
3½" × 3½"
(9 × 9 cm)

B
9½" × 18½"
(24 × 47 cm)

C

A
10½" × 12½"
(26.5 × 31.5 cm)

C

B
10½" × 12½"
(26.5 × 31.5 cm)

A
9½" × 18½"
(24 × 47 cm)

A
3½" × 3½"
(9 × 9 cm)

A
5½" × 8½"
(14 × 21.5 cm)

B
5½" × 8½"
(14 × 21.5 cm)

D
4½" × 5½"
(11.5 × 14 cm)

E

E
4½" × 5½"
(11.5 × 14 cm)

B
5½" × 8½"
(14 × 21.5 cm)

A
5½" × 8½"
(14 × 21.5 cm)

A
9½" × 18½"
(24 × 47 cm)

B
10½" × 12½"
(26.5 × 31.5 cm)

C

A
10½" × 12½"
(26.5 × 31.5 cm)

C

B
9½" × 18½"
(24 × 47 cm)

A
3½" × 3½"
(9 × 9 cm)

B
3½" × 3½"
(9 × 9 cm)

A
12½" × 24½"
(31.5 × 62 cm)

B
12½" × 24½"
(31.5 × 62 cm)

Map Assembly Diagram

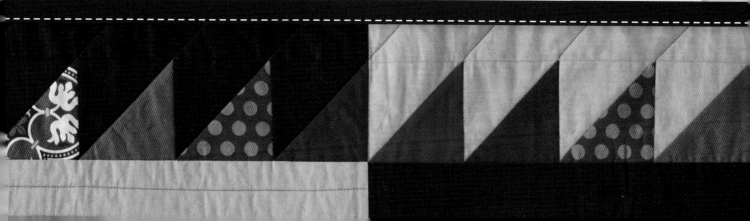

finally a 12½" × 24½" (31.5 × 62 cm) fabric A rectangle to the quarter.

⑦ Make the two B/C/A/E quarters, also as mirror images. Following the assembly diagram on page 63, lay out the half-square triangle blocks into two rows of four B/C blocks and two rows of five B/C blocks. Sew the squares into rows.

⑧ With right sides facing, sew one 3½" (9 cm) fabric B square to one end of each of the two rows with five B/C blocks. Sew each of the two 4½" × 5½" (11.5 × 14 cm) fabric E rectangles to a 5½" × 8½" (14 × 21.5 cm) fabric A rectangle. Sew a 10½" × 12½" (26.5 × 31.5 cm) fabric A rectangle to each pieced rectangle. Add the B/C triangle rows. Add a 9½" × 18½" (24 × 47 cm) fabric B rectangle, then finally a 12½" × 24½" (31.5 × 62 cm) fabric B rectangle.

ASSEMBLE THE TOP

⑨ With right sides facing and matching adjacent seams, sew the four quarters of the quilt together.

FINISH THE QUILT

⑩ Square the quilt top, then pin it to the backing and the batting. Quilt as desired, then add the binding. I quilted Map with straight-line quilting to highlight each section of the quilt. Turn to Tools and Techniques (page 6) for finishing techniques.

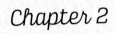

Chapter 2

Special Gifts

All handmade quilts are special, of course. They are all made with love and joy—how can they not be? In this chapter, you will find quilts that are a bit more intriguing in terms of layout and construction. There are corner triangles in different sizes to create allover designs, partial seams to construct a blown-up block on point, unusual triangles as the focus of the design, and thin strips of favorite fabrics inserted in the background.

If you are a jump-in-with-both-feet kind of beginner, you can make these quilts as shown. If you are a more advanced sewist, you will have lots of fun with them by adding your own stamp with color and contrast. Whatever your skill level, these quilts are sure to make anyone receiving them feel extra special. There's that superpower again!

SPARK

FINISHED SIZE
62½" × 80" (159 × 203 cm)

MATERIALS
☐ 5½ yd (5 m) solid navy blue background fabric (A)

☐ ¾ yd (68.5 cm) total red, turquoise, brown, green, chartreuse, black, and white print scraps, at least 18" (45.5 cm) long (B)

☐ 4⅞ yd (4.5 m) backing fabric

☐ ⅔ yd (61 cm) binding fabric

☐ 71" × 88" (180 × 223.5 cm) batting

TOOLS
☐ Basic Sewing Kit (page 6)

Spark is a great way to use leftover trimmings from other quilts for the starbursts. You can also fussy-cut some favorite stripes or high-contrast polka dots.

A dark background shows off bright rays of fabric, but a light background with darker stars would also be striking. Planning the placement of the fabrics and inserting the strips takes time, but this special gift is worth it!

CUT YOUR FABRIC

WOF = width of fabric; LOF = length of fabric

From fabric A:

☐ Cut 2 LOF strips 7" × 63" (18 × 160 cm).

☐ Cut 3 LOF strips 3½" × 63" (9 × 160 cm).

☐ Cut 12 squares 15½" × 15½" (39.5 × 39.5 cm).

☐ Cut 48 squares 2½" × 2½" to 6" × 6" (6.5 × 6.5 cm to 15 × 15 cm), mixing up sizes.

☐ Cut 8 strips 3½" × 15" (9 × 38 cm).

☐ Cut 8 strips 7" × 15" (18 × 38 cm).

From scraps:

☐ Cut 48 strips 1" × 18" (2.5 × 45.5 cm). *Note: If your scraps are not long enough, you can piece the diagonal starburst strips with other scraps.*

The corner triangles are used to vary the length of the diagonal strips, but you can also vary the length of the horizontal and vertical strips before you insert them into the background square.

To piece the strips: Cut the 1" (2.5 cm) wide insert to the length you want plus ½" (1.3 cm). Cut 1" (2.5 cm) wide strips of background fabric. With right sides together, sew the background strips to the ends of the inserts, stitching across the 1" (2.5 cm) width. Use these strips as you do the regular strips.

From binding fabric:

☐ Cut 8 strips 2½" (6.5 cm) × WOF. Trim the selvedges.

SEW THE BLOCKS

Note: All seam allowances are ¼" (6 mm).

① Slice one 15½" (39.5 cm) square in half either straight or at a slight angle (**figure 1**).

② Sew a 1" × 18" (2.5 × 45.5 cm) strip into the slice to insert it. With right sides facing, sew one side of the strip to one cut side of the square. Sew the other strip side to the other square cut side aligning the edges, piecing the square back together with the strip between the two sections.

Trim the ends of the strip that overhang the square (**figure 2**). Press the seams toward the strip.

③ Slice through the square again, almost perpendicular to the first strip, but askew. Following Step 2, sew another strip into the slice (**figure 3**).

④ Slice the square again at a diagonal. Following Step 2, sew a third strip into the cut (**figure 4**).

⑤ Slice again on the remaining diagonal. Following Step 2, sew the last strip into the square and trim the ends even with the square (**figure 5**).

⑥ To create rounded, twinkly stars, use various size fabric A background squares as corner triangles (page 7) on the four corners of the pieced block (**figure 6**).

⑦ Follow Steps 1–6 to make eleven more blocks. Trim each block to 15" (38 cm) square.

ASSEMBLE THE TOP

⑧ With right sides facing, sew one 3½" × 15" (9 × 38 cm) background fabric strip (sashing) between three blocks, alternating block, strip, block, strip, block (as shown in the Spark Assembly Diagram on page 72).

Repeat to make a total of four sashed rows of blocks.

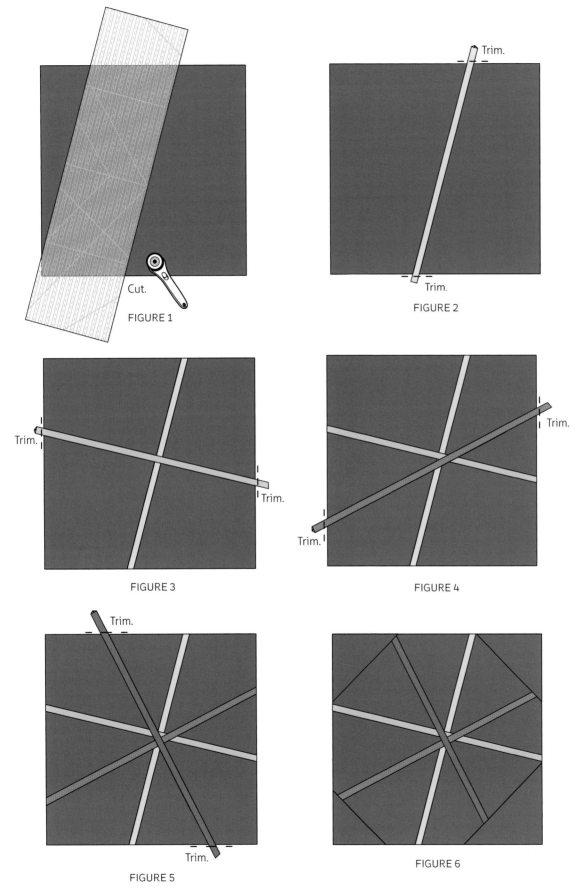

Cut.

FIGURE 1

Trim.

Trim.

FIGURE 2

Trim.

Trim.

FIGURE 3

Trim.

Trim.

FIGURE 4

Trim.

Trim.

FIGURE 5

FIGURE 6

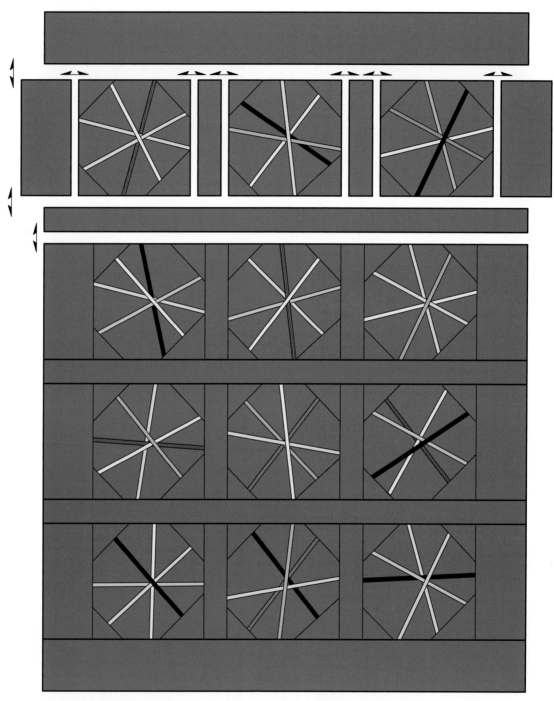

Spark Assembly Diagram

⑨ Following the assembly diagram and with right sides facing, sew one 7" × 15" (18 × 38 cm) background fabric strip to each end of each sashed row and the 3½" × 63" (9 × 160 cm) strips to the bottom edges of three of the rows.

⑩ Sew the rows together in order. Sew one 7" × 63" (18 × 160 cm) background strip to the top and another to the bottom of the quilt top.

FINISH THE QUILT

⑪ Square the quilt top, then pin it to the backing and the batting. Quilt as desired, then add the binding. I quilted Spark in a random, wonky pattern that echos the shape of the stars. Turn to Tools and Techniques (page 6) for finishing techniques.

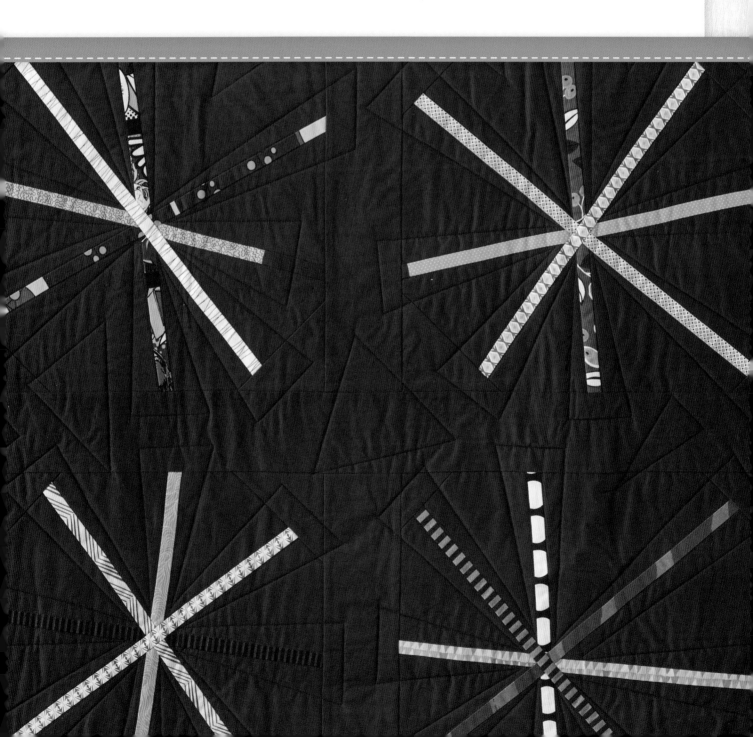

GEM

FINISHED SIZE
63" × 80" (160 × 203 cm)

MATERIALS
- ☐ 3½ yd (3.2 m) solid dark purple fabrics (A)
- ☐ ⅝ yd (57 cm) solid and print light blue fabrics (B)
- ☐ 2½ yd (2.3 m) solid and print green fabrics (C)
- ☐ 5 yd (4.6 m) backing fabric
- ☐ ⅔ yd (61 cm) binding fabric
- ☐ 71" × 88" (180 × 223.5 cm) batting

TOOLS
- ☐ Basic Sewing Kit (page 6)

Corner triangles are a simple way to create a variety of designs. In Gem, they are used extensively in just two sizes to create the form of every block. I used a variety of prints and solids in three groups of closely related colors—deep purple, apple green, and light blue. In the instructions, the fabric quantities are divided into three groups, A, B, and C. You can use just three different fabrics or combine groups of fabrics to meet the yardage requirements, like I did.

You could change the look of Gem completely by using various scraps for each of the corner triangles. Whatever fabrics you choose, Gem is sure to be a sparkling gift for any special person.

CUT YOUR FABRIC

WOF = width of fabric

From fabrics A:

☐ Cut 80 rectangles 6" × 10½"
(15 × 26.5 cm).

From fabrics B:

☐ Cut 80 squares 3" × 3" (7.5 × 7.5 cm).

From fabrics C:

☐ Cut 80 squares 5½" × 5½"
(14 × 14 cm).

☐ Cut 8 strips 2½" (6.5 cm) × WOF.
Trim the selvedges.

From binding fabric:

☐ Cut 8 strips 2½" (6.5 cm) × WOF.
Trim the selvedges.

Tip: If you press your seams to the side, alternate direction so you will be able to match the points more accurately. As you are sewing the four rectangle sections for each block, press the corner triangle seam on half the blocks toward fabric A and press the corner triangle seams on the other half of the blocks away from fabric A.

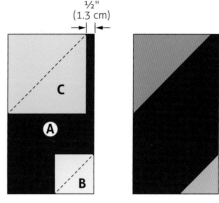

½"
(1.3 cm)

Make 40.

FIGURE 1

½"
(1.3 cm)

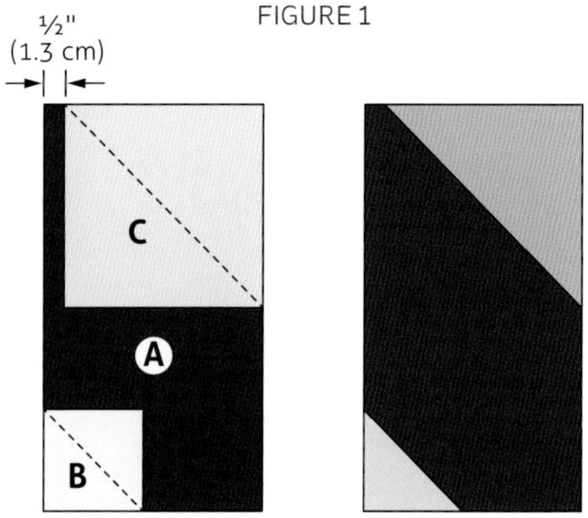

Make 40.

FIGURE 2

SEW THE BLOCKS

Note: All seam allowances are ¼" (6 mm).

① With right sides facing, sew one fabric C square to the top left corner of one fabric A rectangle and one fabric B square to the bottom right corner as corner triangles (page 7). Press seams **(figure 1)**. Make forty.

② With right sides facing, sew one fabric B square to the bottom left corner of a fabric A rectangle and one fabric C square to the top

right corner as corner triangles. Press seams **(figure 2)**. Make forty.

③ With right sides facing, sew two A/B/C rectangles together, matching the two long edges where the fabric B triangles meet **(figure 3)**. Press seam open. Make forty half blocks. Set four half blocks aside.

④ With right sides facing, sew two half blocks together, matching the long edges where the fabric B triangles meet in the middle **(figure 4)**. Press seam open. Make eighteen full blocks.

⑤ With right sides facing, sew two fabric C strips end to end to create one long strip. Trim the strip to 80½" (204.5 cm).

Repeat with the remaining six fabric C strips, making four 80½" (204.5 cm) strips.

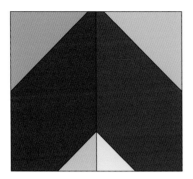

Half block
Make 40.

FIGURE 3

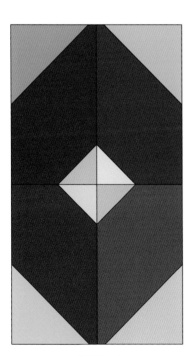

Full block
Make 18.

FIGURE 4

ASSEMBLE THE TOP

⑥ Lay out three columns of four full blocks each. With right sides facing, sew the short sides of four full blocks together.

Repeat to make two more columns.

⑦ Lay out the two alternate columns. With right sides facing, sew the short sides of three full blocks together. Sew one half block onto each end of the column, matching the fabric C corner triangles.

Repeat to make one more column.

⑧ Following the Gem Assembly Diagram, sew the columns together. Start with a full-block column and add a fabric C strip to the right side. Add a half-block column and then another fabric C strip. Repeat, then add the final full-block column.

FINISH THE QUILT

⑨ Square the quilt top, then pin it to the backing and the batting. Quilt as desired, then add the binding. I quilted vertical lines within the block columns and diamonds in the long green strips. Turn to Tools and Techniques (page 6) for finishing techniques.

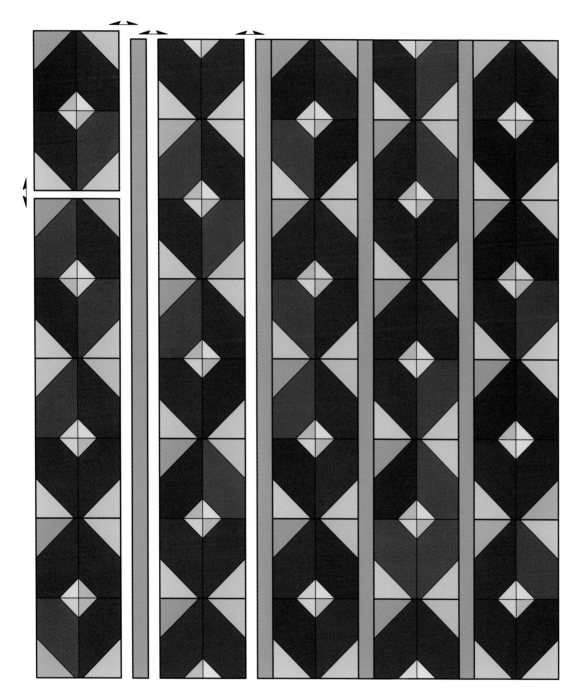

Gem Assembly Diagram

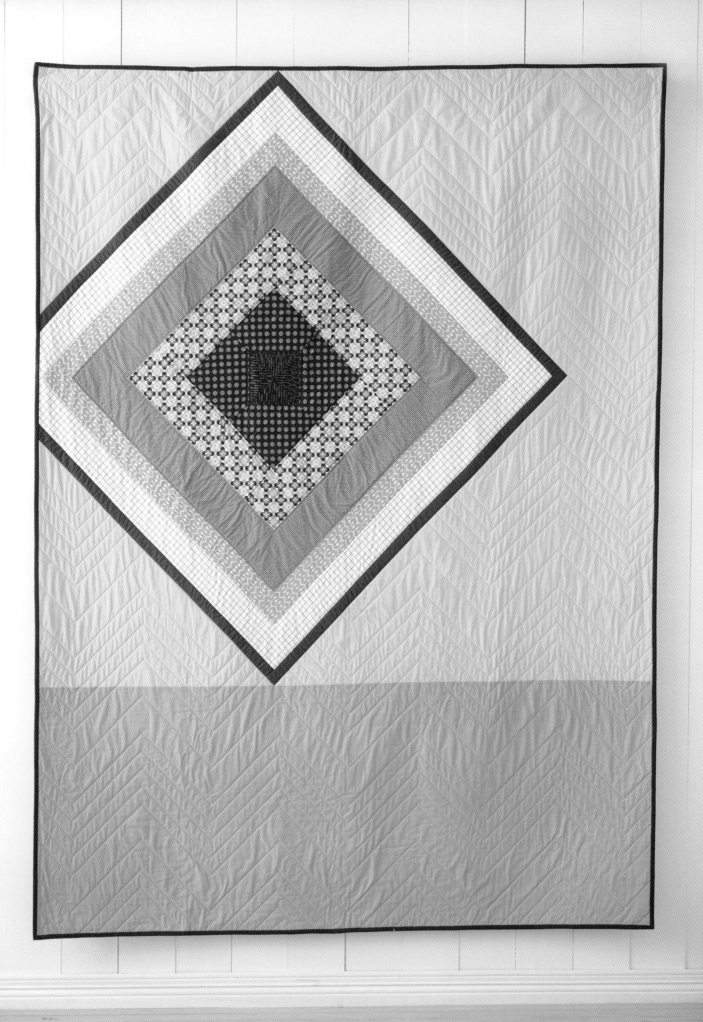

TWINKLE

FINISHED SIZE
60" × 80" (152 × 203 cm)

MATERIALS
- ☐ ¼ yd (23 cm) solid dark red fabric (A)
- ☐ ¼ yd (23 cm) red polka dot fabric (B)
- ☐ ⅜ yd (34.5 cm) coordinating print fabric (C)
- ☐ ⅝ yd (57 cm) solid light red fabric (D)
- ☐ ⅓ yd (30.5 cm) green print fabric (E)
- ☐ ½ yd (45.5 cm) coordinating low-volume print fabric (F)
- ☐ ¼ yd (23 cm) solid medium red fabric (G)
- ☐ 1⅞ yd (1.7 m) solid light yellow fabric (H)
- ☐ 1¾ yd (1.6 m) solid dark yellow fabric (I)
- ☐ 5 yd (4.6 m) backing fabric
- ☐ ⅔ yd (61 cm) binding fabric
- ☐ 68" × 88" (173 × 223.5 cm) batting

TOOLS
- ☐ Basic Sewing Kit (page 6)

Twinkle makes a bold statement with an extra-large block set on point. Although the block could be sewn as a Log Cabin block, with two shorter strips and two longer strips in each concentric square, my oversized Bright Hopes block is used as a simple way to try partial seams. Each of the four strips in each concentric row is cut the same size, making cutting much more efficient. The extra thought it takes to make the partial seams is worth not having twice as many size strips to cut.

Take care not to stretch the long sides of the large background triangles, which are cut on the bias. You can staystitch these sides by sewing them ⅛" (3 mm) from the edge. Twinkle uses four corner triangle blocks in the center of the Bright Hopes block.

CUT YOUR FABRIC

WOF = width of fabric; LOF = length of fabric

From fabric A:

☐ Cut 4 squares 4½" × 4½" (11.5 × 11.5 cm).

From fabric B:

☐ Cut 4 squares 6½" × 6½" (16.5 × 16.5 cm).

From fabric C:

☐ Cut 4 strips 4½" × 16½" (11.5 × 42 cm).

From fabric D:

☐ Cut 4 strips 4½" × 24½" (11.5 × 62 cm).

From fabric E:

☐ Cut 4 strips 2½" × 30½" (6.5 × 77.5 cm).

From fabric F:

☐ Cut 4 strips 3½" × 35½" (9 × 90 cm).

From fabric G:

☐ Cut 4 strips 1½" × 39½" (3.8 × 100.5 cm).

From fabric H:

☐ Cut 1 square 37⅞" × 37⅞" (96 × 96 cm).

☐ Cut 1 square 23⅞" × 23⅞" (61 × 61 cm).

   ▷ Cut the fabric H squares in half once diagonally to create two triangles from each square.

From fabric I:

☐ Cut 1 strip LOF 23½" × 60½" (59.5 × 153.5 cm).

From binding fabric:

☐ Cut 8 strips 2½" (6.5 cm) × WOF. Trim the selvedges.

SEW THE BLOCK

Note: All seam allowances are ¼" (6 mm).

① Sew the oversized Bright Hopes block starting from the center. With right sides facing, make four corner triangles (page 7) using the fabric A and fabric B squares. Pair each square of fabric A with a square of fabric B, positioning a corner of fabric A into a corner of fabric B (**figure 1**).

② With right sides facing, stitch two of the squares together with the fabric A triangles touching. Stitch the remaining two squares together also with the fabric A triangles touching. Sew the stitched pieces together to create a larger square with all of the fabric A triangles meeting in the center (**figure 2**).

③ Sew the rows around the center square, beginning each row with a partial seam. Sew one strip of fabric C to one side of the center square, sewing only ¾ of the way down the side of the center square. Press fabric C open.

Working counterclockwise around the center square, sew the second strip of fabric C to the center square, continuing over the short end of the first strip. Sew the third strip of fabric C to the center square and short end of the second strip. Sew the last strip of fabric C to the center square and short end of the third strip. Finish sewing the seam of the first strip (**figure 3**).

④ Following Step 3, continue sewing the fabric D, E, F, and G rows around the center.

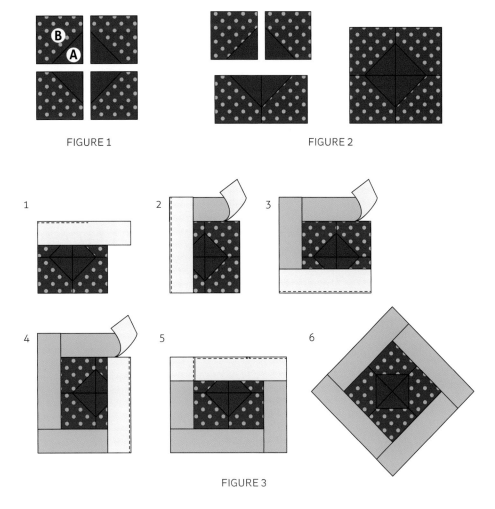

FIGURE 1

FIGURE 2

FIGURE 3

FIGURE 4

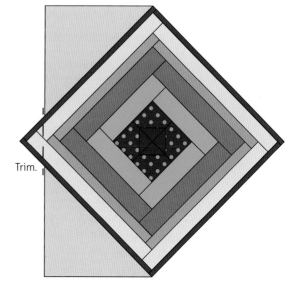

FIGURE 5

ASSEMBLE THE TOP

⑤ Turn the Bright Hopes block on point and add the first piece of background fabric. Attach the long side of one small fabric H triangle to the upper left side of the block, matching the top point of the square to the point of the triangle. Part of the block will extend beyond the side of the triangle (**figure 4**).

⑥ Attach the long side of the second small background triangle to the lower left side of the center block, matching the bottom point of the block to the point of the triangle. Part of the Bright Hopes block will extend beyond the side of the triangle (**figure 5**).

⑦ Trim the point of the primary block even with the triangles (**figure 6**).

⑧ Sew the long side of one large fabric H triangle to the lower right side of the primary block, matching the bottom point of the block to the point of the triangle. This time,

the triangle will extend beyond the side of the block. Trim the point of the triangle that extends beyond the square even with the perpendicular side of the block (**figure 7**).

⑨ Sew the second large fabric H triangle to the upper right side of the center block, continuing along the trimmed portion of the adjacent triangle (**figure 8**).

⑩ Sew the fabric I rectangle to the bottom of the quilt top (**figure 9**).

FINISH THE QUILT

⑪ Square the quilt top, then pin it to the backing and the batting. Quilt as desired, then add the binding. I echo-quilted the square in Twinkle. The yellow background was quilted in large zigzags to mimic the on-point orientation of the block. Turn to Tools and Techniques (page 6) for finishing techniques.

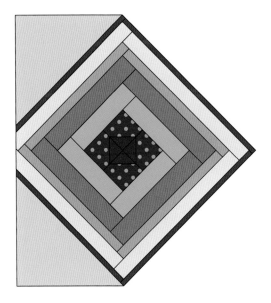

FIGURE 6

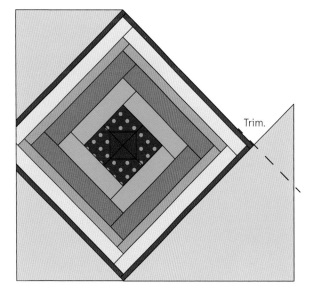

Trim.

FIGURE 7

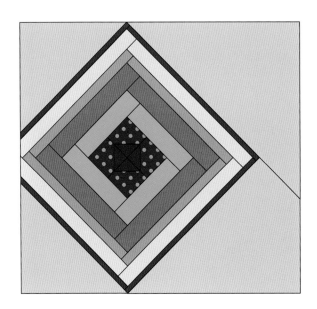

FIGURE 8

FIGURE 9

WAVE

FINISHED SIZE
62" × 77½" (157.5 × 197 cm)

MATERIALS
- ☐ 3 yd (2.75 m) total blue print and solid fabrics (A)
- ☐ 3 yd (2.75 m) total orange print and solid fabrics (B)
- ☐ 5 yd (4.6 m) backing fabric
- ☐ ⅝ yd (57 cm) binding fabric
- ☐ 70" × 86" (178 × 218 cm) batting
- ☐ 1 sheet of template plastic

TOOLS
- ☐ Basic Sewing Kit (page 6)
- ☐ Wave template (page 139)

Wave is a very versatile design that transforms with your choice of colors. With only one size and shape of pieces to cut, Wave allows you to focus on color and placement. The pattern manifests as a landscape, zigzags, flags, or any number of geometric and graphic images, depending on where you place those colors. The flexibility of Wave allows you to create a special gift for anyone on your list.

Here, I used two main color families, blue and orange, with a variety of strong tints and shades within each family. Blue and orange are directly opposite each other on the color wheel. You might try other complementary color combinations, such as yellows and purples or reds with greens. Try your favorite negative-space neutral with a bold accent fabric or choose multiple tones of just one color family for a more subtle look.

CUT YOUR FABRIC

WOF = width of fabric

Copy the Wave template (page 139), trace it onto template plastic, and cut it out.

From fabrics A and B each:

☐ Cut 12 strips 8½" (21.5 cm) × WOF. Trim the selvedges.

> ▷ Line up the short edge of the triangle template with one long edge of one 8½" (21.5 cm) strip. Point A of the triangle should touch the opposite edge of the fabric (**figure 1**).

> ▷ Cut 7 triangles from the strip. Turn the template 180° with each new cut (**figure 2**).

> ▷ Continue cutting triangles until you have 84 triangles of each color.

From binding fabric:

☐ Cut 7 strips 2½" (6.5 cm) × WOF. Trim the selvedges.

SEW THE BLOCKS

Note: All seam allowances are ¼" (6 mm).

① To sew the triangles together, sew one long edge of a fabric A triangle to one long edge of a fabric B triangle, alternating direction.

In this way, sew twenty-one triangles together, alternating fabric A with fabric B to create the first column. Start and end the column with a fabric A triangle (**figure 3**).

Make a total of four identical A columns.

② Make four more columns of twenty-one alternating triangles, but start and end them with a fabric B triangle (**figure 4**). These are the B columns.

ASSEMBLE THE TOP

③ Trim each column square on both short ends. Cut each end triangle ¼" (6 mm) beyond point A, perpendicular to the long sides of the column (**figure 5**).

FIGURE 1

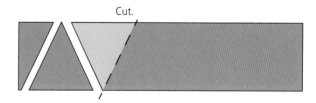

FIGURE 2

Column A
Make 4.

FIGURE 3

Column B
Make 4.

FIGURE 4

¼"
(6 mm)

Trim.

FIGURE 5

④ With right sides facing, sew the columns. Follow the Wave Assembly Diagram for placement and orientation.

FINISH THE QUILT

⑤ Square the quilt top, then pin it to the backing and batting. Quilt as desired, then add the binding. For Wave, I mimicked the triangles by quilting random zigzags throughout the quilt in two different thread colors. Turn to Tools and Techniques (page 6) for finishing techniques.

Column B   Column A   Column A   Column B   Column B   Column A   Column A   Column B

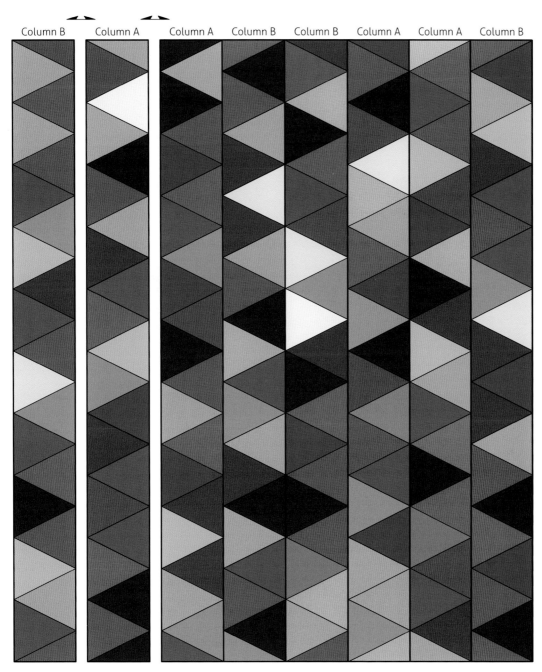

Wave Assembly Diagram

ECHO

FINISHED SIZE
67" × 77" (170 × 196 cm)

MATERIALS
- ☐ ¾ yd (68.5 cm) low-volume yellow print fabric (A)
- ☐ ¾ yd (68.5 cm) orange stripe fabric (B)
- ☐ 1⅛ yd (1.03 m) solid pale lime fabric (C)
- ☐ ¾ yd (68.5 cm) orange polka dot fabric (D)
- ☐ ¾ yd (68.5 cm) navy blue polka dot fabric (E)
- ☐ ⅜ yd (34.5 cm) turquoise print fabric (F)
- ☐ ¼ yd (23 cm) lime stripe fabric (G)
- ☐ 4¾ yd (4.4 m) backing fabric
- ☐ ⅝ yd (57 cm) binding fabric
- ☐ 75" × 85" (190.5 × 216 cm) batting

TOOLS
- ☐ Basic Sewing Kit (page 6)

This double-symmetry quilt may look complex, but it is simply pieced with eight rectangular blocks made from three identical triangles and three mirror-image triangles. It is great fun to play around with the placement of the triangles, such as creating a pinwheel, to break up the symmetry.

Color and print choices will certainly allow for many different looks for this quilt—contrasting solids will create a high-impact quilt, while floral prints could make a bold bouquet. The materials list calls for seven different fabrics for the top, but you can use less. Combine fabric quantities to make sure you will have enough yardage.

CUT YOUR FABRIC

WOF = width of fabric

From fabrics A, B, D, and E each:

☐ Cut 4 rectangles 11⅝" × 20" (29.5 × 51 cm).

From fabric C:

☐ Cut 6 rectangles 11⅝" × 20" (29.5 × 51 cm).

From fabric F:

☐ Cut 2 rectangles 11⅝" × 20" (29.5 × 51 cm).

▷ Cut all of the rectangles in half once diagonally.

Because you are making a symmetrical design, you must make half of the triangles of each fabric go in one direction and half go in the other direction. If your fabric is reversible, such as a woven solid, you can cut all the triangles in the same direction and flip half of them over. If you have one-sided fabric, you will need to cut half of the rectangles of each fabric into triangles diagonally in one direction **(figure 1)** and half of the rectangles of each fabric into triangles diagonally in the other direction **(figure 2)**.

From fabric G:

☐ Cut 4 squares 6⅞" × 6⅞" (17.5 × 17.5 cm).

From binding fabric:

☐ Cut 8 strips 2½" (6.5 cm) × WOF. Trim the selvedges.

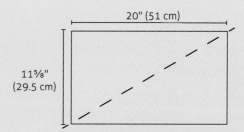

20" (51 cm)	20" (51 cm)
11⅝" (29.5 cm)	11⅝" (29.5 cm)

Cut half of the rectangles of each fabric from the top left corner to the bottom right corner.

FIGURE 1

Cut half of the rectangles of each fabric from the top right corner to the bottom left corner.

FIGURE 2

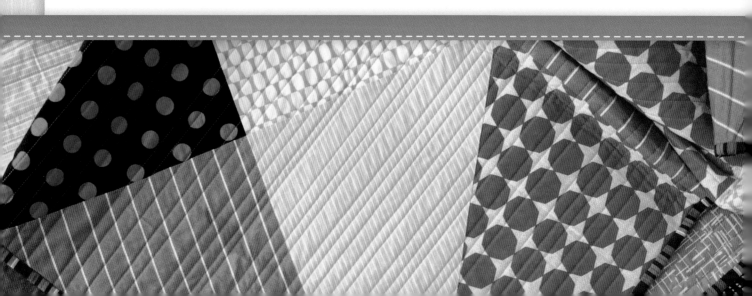

In two places, twelve points will come together. Keep track of which direction you are pressing the seams, so they will all go around in the same direction to help reduce bulk.

SEW THE BLOCKS

Note: All seam allowances are ¼" (6 mm).

① Sew the triangles together to make eight rectangular blocks as shown in **figure 3**.

For blocks A and B, sew triangle F to triangle E, then add triangle D. Sew triangle B to triangle A, then add triangle C. Sew the two units together along the D/E and A/C edges.

For blocks C and D, sew triangle C to triangle E, then add triangle A. Sew triangle D to triangle C, then add triangle B. Sew the two units together along the A/E and C/B edges.

Make two each of blocks A, B, C, and D to make the mirror image. Blocks A and B create the center with the fabric G corner triangles all coming together. Blocks C and D complete the top and bottom of the quilt.

Before you start assembling the top, lay out the triangles carefully to make sure you have the pieces oriented correctly.

② To finish the four A and B blocks, add one fabric G square as a corner triangle (page 7) to each fabric F triangle.

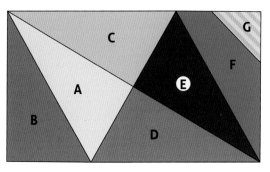

Block A
Make 2.

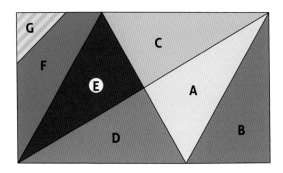

Block B
Make 2.

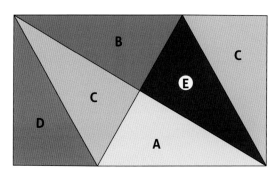

Block C
Make 2.

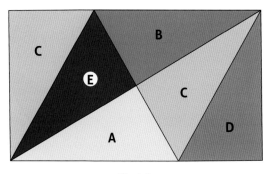

Block D
Make 2.

FIGURE 3

ASSEMBLE THE TOP

③ Following the Echo Assembly Diagram, rotate one of each of the four different blocks 180°. Sew the eight blocks together to create the double-symmetry quilt top.

FINISH THE QUILT

④ Square the quilt top, then pin it to the backing and the batting. Quilt as desired, then add the binding. I used randomly spaced vertical lines to keep it simple and let the graphic pattern and bold colors shine. Turn to Tools and Techniques (page 6) for finishing techniques.

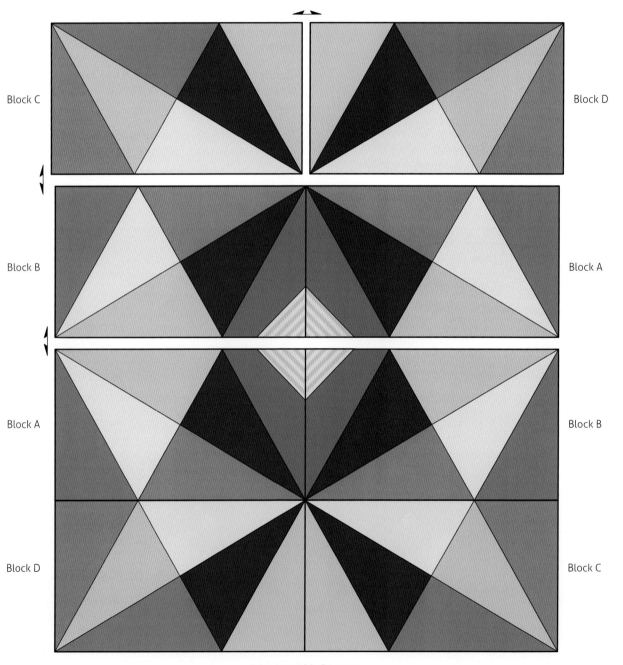

Echo Assembly Diagram

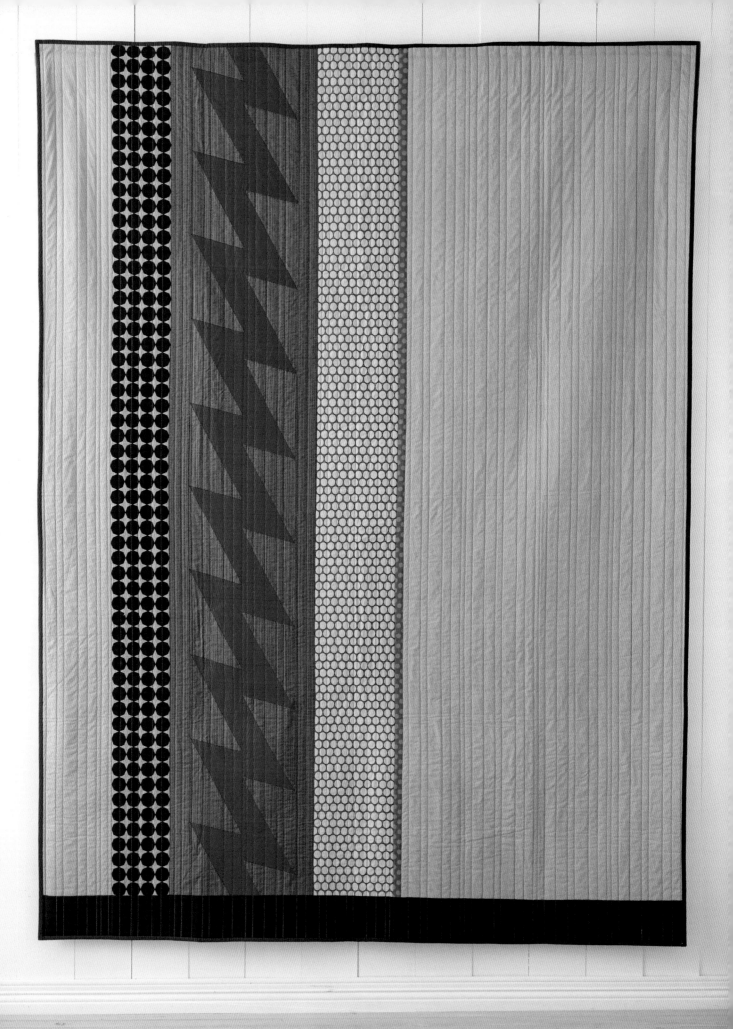

BOLT

FINISHED SIZE
63¾" × 84" (162 × 213 cm)

MATERIALS
- ☐ ⅞ yd (80 cm) solid dark gray fabric (A)
- ☐ ⅝ yd (57 cm) solid red fabric (B)
- ☐ 2⅛ yd (1.9 m) solid light gray fabric (C)
- ☐ ⅝ yd (57 cm) yellow-and-gray polka dot fabric (D)
- ☐ ⅜ yd (34.5 cm) black-and-gray polka dot fabric (E)
- ☐ ⅛ yd (11.5 cm) turquoise polka dot fabric (F)
- ☐ ⅜ yd (34.5 cm) solid black fabric (G)
- ☐ 5¼ yd (4.8 m) backing fabric
- ☐ ⅔ yd (61 cm) binding fabric
- ☐ 72" × 92" (183 × 234 cm) batting
- ☐ 1 sheet of template plastic

TOOLS
- ☐ Basic Sewing Kit (page 6)
- ☐ Bolt template (page 138)

Bolt is a simple quilt, yet it allows you to have some fun with the lightning-bolt design. This graphic quilt is great practice for trying out a new triangle shape, but you can use a single strip of fabric or a row of your favorite blocks instead. However you decide to sew Bolt, choosing bold colors and surprising accents, such as a bright blue binding, will make this minimal quilt a special gift.

Use the template provided to cut the lightning-bolt pieces. When cutting out the triangles for the lightning bolt, be sure that your triangles are all facing in the correct direction. You are cutting the same triangle repeatedly, not mirror images.

CUT YOUR FABRIC

WOF = width of fabric

From fabric A:

☐ Cut 3 strips 6" × 40" (15 × 101.5 cm).

☐ Cut 4 strips 2½" (6.5 cm) × WOF. Trim the selvedges.

From fabric B:

☐ Cut 3 strips 6" × 40" (15 × 101.5 cm).

From fabric C:

☐ Cut 2 strips 28" (71 cm) × WOF. Trim the selvedges.

☐ Cut 2 strips 7½" (19 cm) × WOF. Trim the selvedges.

From fabric D:

☐ Cut 2 strips 8½" (21.5 cm) × WOF. Trim the selvedges.

From fabric E:

☐ Cut 2 strips 6" (15 cm) × WOF. Trim the selvedges.

From fabric F:

☐ Cut 2 strips 1½" (3.8 cm) × WOF. Trim the selvedges.

From fabric G:

☐ Cut 2 strips 4½" (11.5 cm) × WOF. Trim the selvedges.

From binding fabric:

☐ Cut 8 strips 2½" (6.5 cm) × WOF. Trim the selvedges.

CUT THE TRIANGLES

① Lay one of the fabric A or B strips in front of you vertically. You will cut the lowermost triangle and work your way to the top of the strip.

Trace the template onto template plastic and cut it out; transfer all the markings to the plastic. Line up side A with the left long edge of the fabric. Cut along sides B and C to make the first triangle **(figure 1)**.

② Turn the template 180° and match side A with the right long edge of the fabric. Cut along side B to make the second triangle **(figure 2)**.

③ Following Steps 1 and 2, continue to turn the template and cut the remainder of the triangles with all the fabric A and B 6" × 40" (15 × 101.5 cm) lightning-bolt strips. You will have twenty-two fabric A triangles and twenty-two fabric B triangles.

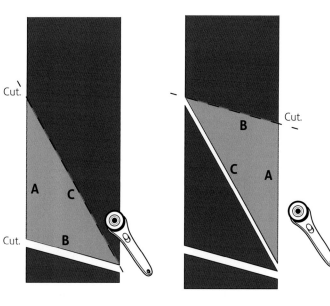

FIGURE 1   FIGURE 2

SEW THE BLOCKS

Note: All seam allowances are ¼" (6 mm).

④ To sew the lightning bolt, match each of the fabric A triangles to one of the fabric B triangles. Lay out the sets matching the long diagonal edges to form a parallelogram (not a kite shape) **(figure 3)**.

Place the triangles right sides facing and sew the diagonal seam. Press seam open. Make twenty-two parallelogram blocks.

⑤ With right sides facing, sew eleven blocks together into a strip, matching the short ends of the parallelograms **(figure 4)**.

Repeat with the other eleven parallelograms to make a second identical strip.

⑥ Turn one strip 180°. Place it next to the other strip so that the fabric B triangles are next to each other. Shift the strips so the points of the fabric A triangles are near the center of the B triangles, creating a zigzagged lightning bolt **(figure 5)**.

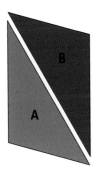

Make 22.

FIGURE 3

Make 2.

FIGURE 4

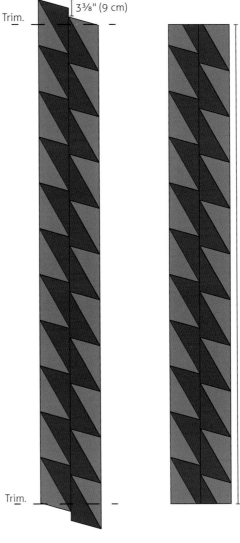

Trim.

3⅜" (9 cm)

Trim.

80½" (204.5 cm)

FIGURE 5

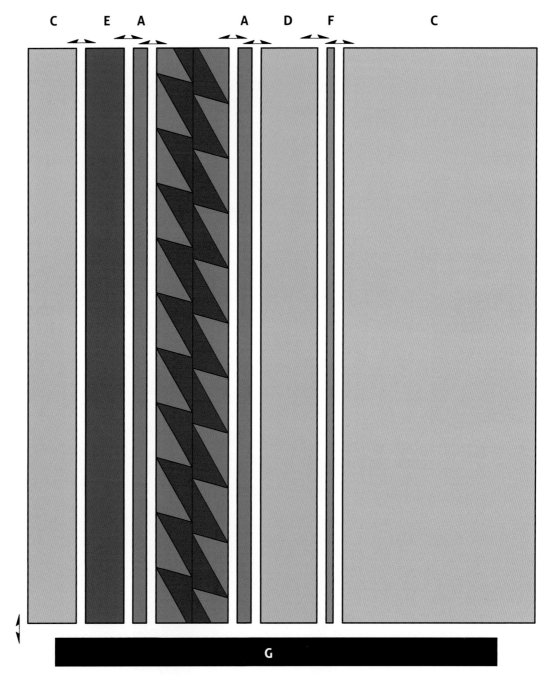

Bolt Assembly Diagram

With right sides facing, sew the two strips together.

⑦ Trim about 3⅜" (9 cm) off of each end of the lightning-bolt strip. It should measure 80½" (204.5 cm) long.

⑧ With right sides facing, complete the other strips for the top, matching like-size rectangles: A with A, etc.

Sew each pair of strips together across the short ends of the strips. Make two long strips of fabric A, two different-width strips of fabric C, and one strip each of fabrics D, E, F, and G.

⑨ Cut the strips from fabrics A, B, C, D, E, and F to 80½" (204.5 cm) long.

Cut the fabric G strip to 63¾" (162 cm) long.

ASSEMBLE THE TOP

⑩ Assemble the quilt top, sewing the strips right sides together in order according to the Bolt Assembly Diagram. Press the seams in one direction.

⑪ With right sides facing, sew the fabric G rectangle along the bottom of the quilt top.

FINISH THE QUILT

⑫ Square the top, then pin it to the backing and batting. Quilt as desired, then add the binding. I quilted Bolt with randomly spaced vertical lines. Turn to Tools and Techniques (page 6) for finishing techniques.

BLOOM

FINISHED SIZE
78" × 84½" (198 × 215 cm)

MATERIALS
- ☐ 3¾ yd (3.4 m) brown print fabric (A)
- ☐ 1½ yd (137 cm) solid purple fabric (B)
- ☐ 1 yd (91.5 cm) purple polka dot fabric (C)
- ☐ ¼ yd (23 cm) solid yellow fabric (D)
- ☐ ¼ yd (23 cm) solid green fabric (E)
- ☐ ¼ yd (23 cm) solid orange fabric (F)
- ☐ 7¼ yd (6.6 m) backing fabric
- ☐ ¾ yd (68.5 cm) binding fabric
- ☐ 86" × 93" (218 × 236 cm) batting

TOOLS
- ☐ Basic Sewing Kit (page 6)

Extra-large blocks create instant drama. The blocks in Bloom run right off the edges of the quilt to increase the impact. I love a dark fabric for negative space to let the colors sparkle. Bloom would also be lovely in low-volume fabrics and wild florals. The offset layout requires a bit of planning, but makes this gift unique.

The angles in Bloom are all created simply by cutting squares and sewing them as corner triangles. You will have lots of trimmings from the corner triangles, so save them for scrappy quilts and fabric collages.

CUT YOUR FABRIC

WOF = width of fabric

From fabric A:

☐ Cut 22 squares 7" × 7" (18 × 18 cm).

☐ Cut 4 squares 20" × 20" (51 × 51 cm).

☐ Cut 6 rectangles 13½" × 20" (34.5 × 51 cm).

☐ Cut 4 rectangles 7" × 20" (18 × 51 cm).

☐ Cut 4 rectangles 7" × 13½" (18 × 34.5 cm).

From fabric B:

☐ Cut 40 squares 7" × 7" (18 × 18 cm).

From fabric C:

☐ Cut 24 squares 7" × 7" (18 × 18 cm).

From fabric D:

☐ Cut 44 squares 2½" × 2½" (6.5 × 6.5 cm).

From fabric E:

☐ Cut 20 squares 2½" × 2½" (6.5 × 6.5 cm).

From fabric F:

☐ Cut 5 squares 7" × 7" (18 × 18 cm).

From binding fabric:

☐ Cut 9 strips 2½" (6.5 cm) × WOF. Trim the selvedges.

Make 5.

FIGURE 1

Make 22.

FIGURE 2

Make 12.

FIGURE 3

SEW THE BLOCKS

Note: All seam allowances are ¼" (6 mm).

① Sew a fabric E square as a corner triangle (page 7) on each corner of the five fabric F squares **(figure 1)**.

② Sew a fabric D square as a corner triangle on two adjacent corners on each of the twenty-two 7" (18 cm) fabric A squares **(figure 2)**.

③ Sew a fabric C square to the top and bottom of a fabric A pieced square from Step 2 **(figure 3)**. Make twelve units total.

④ Sew a fabric B square as a corner triangle on each corner of the four 20" (51 cm) fabric A squares **(figure 4)**.

⑤ Sew a fabric B square as a corner triangle on two of the long-side adjacent corners of each of the six 13½" × 20" (34.5 × 51 cm) fabric A rectangles **(figure 5)**.

⑥ Sew a fabric B square as a corner triangle on two of the long-side adjacent corners of each of the four 7" × 20" (18 × 51 cm) fabric A rectangles **(figure 6)**.

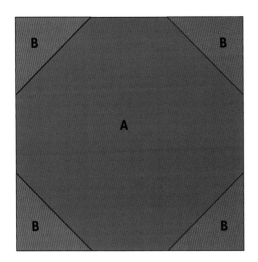

Make 4.

FIGURE 4

Make 6.

FIGURE 5

Make 4.

FIGURE 6

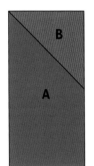

Make 2.

Make 2.

FIGURE 7

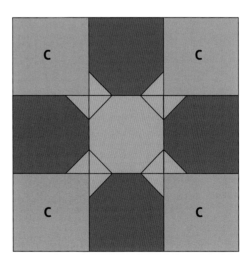

FIGURE 8

⑦ Sew a fabric B square as a corner triangle onto one upper corner of each of the four 7" × 13½" (18 × 34.5 cm) fabric A rectangles. On two of the rectangles, place the corner triangles on the upper right corner. On the remaining two rectangles, place the corner triangles on the upper left corner in a mirror image of the first two **(figure 7)**.

⑧ Assemble the flower centers. Make a nine-patch block for each of the five flowers using a fabric F/E square and two fabric A/D squares in the center column and the fabric A/D/C units on the sides **(figure 8)**.

ASSEMBLE THE TOP

⑨ Sew the blocks into rows, orienting the corner triangles to create the flower pattern.

For rows 1 and 5, start with a 7" × 20" (18 × 51 cm) fabric A/B rectangle, add a nine-patch flower center, a 20" (51 cm) fabric A/B square, another nine-patch flower center, and finally another 7" × 20" (18 × 51 cm) fabric A/B rectangle (figure 9).

⑩ For row 3, start with a fabric A/C/D rectangle, add a 20" (51 cm) fabric A/B square, a nine-patch flower, another 20" (51 cm) fabric A/B square, and another fabric A/C/D rectangle (figure 10).

⑪ For rows 2 and 4, start with a 7" × 13½" (18 × 34.5 cm) fabric A/B rectangle, add three 13½" × 20" (34.5 × 51 cm) fabric A/B rectangles, and finish with a 7" × 13½" (18 × 34.5 cm) fabric A/B rectangle. Take care to orient the rectangles so that the corner triangles create the flower pattern (figure 11).

⑫ Sew the rows together in numerical order, following the Bloom Assembly Diagram.

FINISH THE QUILT

⑬ Square the top, then pin it to the batting and the backing. Quilt as desired, then add the binding. I used careful echo and straight-line quilting in the center of each flower block to contrast with the wonky lightning-bolt quilting in the remainder of the quilt. Turn to Tools and Techniques (page 6) for finishing techniques.

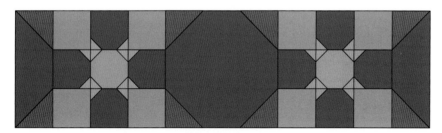

Rows 1 and 5
Make 2.

FIGURE 9

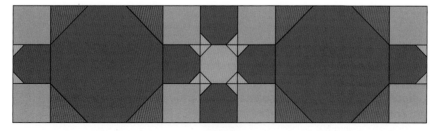

Row 3
Make 1.

FIGURE 10

Rows 2 and 4
Make 2.

FIGURE 11

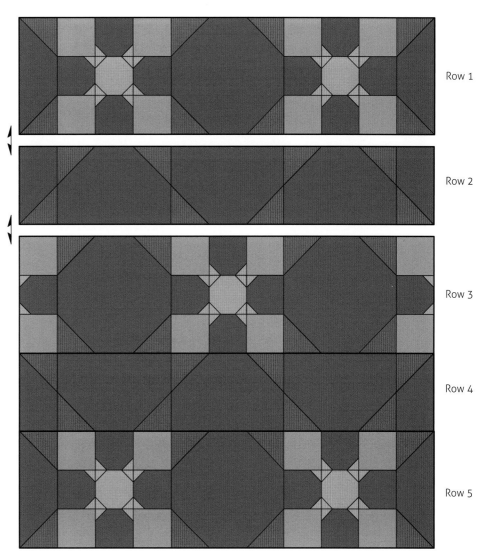

Row 1

Row 2

Row 3

Row 4

Row 5

Bloom Assembly Diagram

Chapter 3

Group Gifts

Group quilts have an amazing ability to spread joy exponentially. What fun that a sewist from New Zealand can send a quilt block around the world to be part of a bee quilt with blocks from Switzerland, France, and every corner of the United States. How fortunate I have been to be part of a local community of generous quilters and non-quilters who want to help share handmade quilts through my Bright Hopes organization.

Whether you are part of a family sewing a quilt for a loved one, a local bee sewing a gift, or a group of like-minded strangers making a quilt to donate, these group quilts can be made successfully by all skill levels. Use up long thin leftover strips, give freedom to each sewist over her block contribution, construct long border sections instead of blocks, and insert a little individuality in each block with fun trims. Whatever quilts you decide to make with your group, your recipient will feel the extra love. Superheroes unite!

CIRCUS

FINISHED SIZE
58½" × 82" (148.5 × 208 cm)

MATERIALS
- ☐ ⅛ yd (11.5 cm) each of 60 solid colors (A)
- ☐ ½ yd (45.5 cm) ½" wide rickrack*
- ☐ ½ yd (45.5 cm) ball fringe*
- ☐ ⅛ yd (11 cm) of scraps for prairie points*
- ☐ 1¾ yd (1.6 m) white sashing fabric (B)
- ☐ 5 yd (4.6 m) backing fabric
- ☐ ⅔ yd (61 cm) binding fabric
- ☐ 67" × 90" (170 × 229cm) batting
- ☐ Embroidery floss

Amount required for each insertion. You can insert as many trims as desired in any or all of the blocks.

TOOLS
- ☐ Basic Sewing Kit (page 6)
- ☐ Zipper foot

A bee, online or in person, is a perfect forum for creating Circus. This simple quilt uses bright solids and fun trims as inserts. True beginners can leave out the inserts and make a simple striped block. Advanced quilters can add an assortment of points and trims between the stripes. Highlight the bold blocks with crisp white sashing like I did or use a fun print to set off the solids.

If you make Circus with your online bee group, be sure to specify your color preferences or send the fabrics you would like participants to use.

CUT YOUR FABRIC

WOF = width of fabric; LOF = length of fabric

From fabric A (mixing up the colors in various sizes):

☐ Cut 24 strips 4½" × 16½" (11.5 × 42 cm).

☐ Cut 24 strips 3½" × 16½" (9 × 42 cm).

☐ Cut 12 strips 2½" × 16½" (6.5 × 42 cm).

From fabric B:

☐ Cut 3 LOF strips 6½" × 60½" (16.5 × 154 cm).

☐ Cut 8 LOF strips 6½" × 16½" (16.5 × 42 cm).

From binding fabric:

☐ Cut 8 strips 2½" (6.5 cm) × WOF. Trim off selvedges.

Tip: When cutting and sewing trims, be careful not to stretch them! Once they are sewn in, they can retract like elastic and make the fabric distort and pucker.

PREPARE THE TRIMS

① **Rickrack:** Cut a 17" (43 cm) length. Plan for the stitching to go right down the center of the rickrack length. Measure half of the width of the rickrack, the distance from the center of the trim to the edge. If it is more than ¼" (6 mm), trim the length of one side to ¼" (6 mm) **(figure 1)**.

② **Ball fringe:** Cut a 17" (43 cm) length. Leaving the woven header strip, cut off any pom-poms that are within 2" (5 cm) of either end **(figure 2)**.

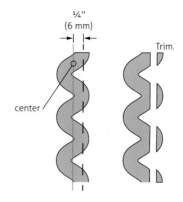

FIGURE 1

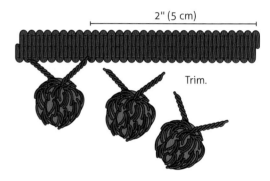

FIGURE 2

③ **Prairie points:** Cut six 2½" (6.5 cm) squares of assorted fabrics. Fold the squares in half to make a rectangle. With the folded edge on top, fold the two top corners to meet in the middle of the bottom edge, and press **(figure 3)**.

SEW THE BLOCKS

Note: All seam allowances are ¼" (6 mm).

④ Sort the strips into twelve block sets. Each set must include two 4½" × 16½" (11.5 × 42 cm) strips, two 3½" × 16½" (9 × 42 cm)strips, and one 2½" × 16½" (6.5 × 42 cm) strip.

⑤ Lay out the strips in any order you choose and insert the trims into whatever seams you like.

Rickrack: Position the length of trim on one long edge of a fabric strip. There should be about a ¼" (6 mm) overhang on each end. With right sides facing, place another fabric strip on top, with the rickrack between. Pin, then sew down the length of the seam. Press the seam to one side. The rickrack will lay on the opposite fabric on the right side of the block.

Ball fringe: Lay the fringe on one long edge of a fabric strip, matching the woven header to the fabric edge. Take each woven end of the ball fringe and curve it down past the edge of the fabric. Baste the ball fringe onto the fabric strip with a ⅛" (3 mm) seam **(figure 4)**.

With right sides facing, place another fabric strip on top and, using a zipper foot, sew down the length of the seam. Press the seam to one side. The ball fringe will lay on the right side on the opposite fabric.

Prairie points: Match the edges of the prairie points to one long edge of a fabric strip. Keep the inserts at least 1" (2.5 cm) away from the ends of the fabric strips. Baste or pin the inserts in place. With right sides together, place another fabric strip on top and sew down the length of the seam. Press the seam to one side. The inserts will lay on the right side on the opposite fabric.

⑥ With right sides facing, sew the rest of the strips together to finish the square block **(figure 5)**.

⑦ Follow Steps 5 and 6 to sew the remaining 11 blocks in the same manner.

ASSEMBLE THE TOP

⑧ Following the Circus Assembly Diagram on page 116, sew together three blocks alternately with two 6½" × 16½"(16.5 × 42 cm) sashing strips.

Repeat to sew four rows.

⑨ Attach the 6½" × 60½" (16.5 × 154 cm) sashing strips to the bottom of three rows. Sew the rows together to complete the quilt top.

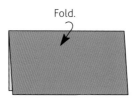

Fold.

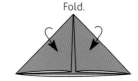

Fold.

FIGURE 3

⌐ ⅛" (3 mm)

FIGURE 4

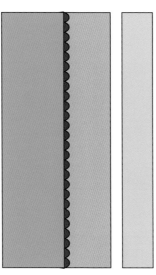
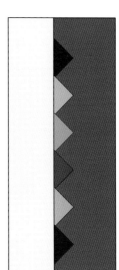

FIGURE 5

FINISH THE QUILT

⑩ Square the top, then pin it to the batting and the backing. Quilt as desired, then add the binding. I did straight-line quilting in the sashing. For the blocks, I used straight-line zigzags in some of the strips and hand quilting with embroidery floss in others. Turn to Tools and Techniques (page 6) for finishing techniques.

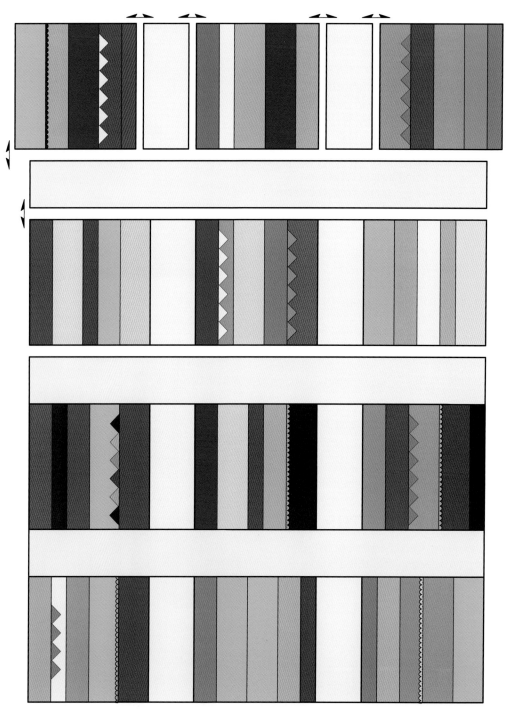

Circus Assembly Diagram

Gather Together

My work with the nonprofit Bright Hopes Collaborative Quilt Project has enabled me to work with many wonderful community groups. Whether you are working with a local group (quilt group or otherwise) or an online sewing bee, the quilts you make together can be some of the most dynamic, wonderful, and often unexpected and interesting quilts you will ever make.

Among the projects in this book, the quilts in this chapter are designed to make with groups. These quilts are constructed in blocks or sections that can be sewn by individuals and then brought together to create the completed quilt.

Garden (page 124) is constructed of borders instead of blocks. There are four different lengths, so you can divide the work according to how much time participants can give or assign shorter lengths to beginner sewists. Picnic (page 118) consists of twenty-four similar blocks; make them in the same colorway, but give the members of your group some individual freedom when choosing fabrics. Both Picnic and Garden were pieced by members of Bright Hopes.

Nest (page 130) is a flexible quilt that works well with groups of new sewists. To make my version, the scrappy improvisational blocks were sewn by adults at a local day-treatment program. This format gave the participants freedom to choose and place fabrics creatively. It is very forgiving. The blocks were then trimmed and completed with sashing by Bright Hopes members.

Similarly, Circus was pieced by an online group called Stash Bee. Using solid fabrics in Circus made it simple for everyone to complete blocks without having to purchase more fabric or for me, as the quilt leader for the month, having to send fabric around the world to get the blocks I wanted.

When working with a community group, preparation is key. How many participants will there be? Your quilt will change depending on if there are five participants or seventy-five. Piecing blocks is important, but who will assemble the top and who will do the quilting? At Bright Hopes, we make many tops with new sewists, but often ask the experienced sewers among our volunteers to help with the quilting.

Be sure to use a system that will work for you and whatever group you are working with. Whether you are sewing with close family or strangers around the world, be flexible and encouraging, and you and your group are sure to have great fun.

PICNIC

FINISHED SIZE
60" × 90" (152 × 229 cm)

MATERIALS
- ☐ 4 yd (3.7 m) total red print fabrics (A)
- ☐ 3¾ yd (3.4 m) total yellow print fabrics (B)
- ☐ ½ yd (45.5 cm) total purple print fabrics (C)
- ☐ 5⅝ yd (5.2 m) backing fabric
- ☐ ⅔ yd (61 cm) binding fabric
- ☐ 68" × 98" (173 × 249 cm) batting
- ☐ Foundation paper such as unprinted newsprint (optional)

TOOLS
- ☐ Basic Sewing Kit (page 6)
- ☐ Walking foot (optional)

I save every scrap of leftover fabric. Scraps are perfect for sewing into new quilts, and they are especially fun to sew with a group for a collaborative project. Scrap quilts are very forgiving. If a scrap is not long enough, add another scrap onto it. If a scrap is too big, just cut it off. Choose three main colors for this quilt—red, yellow, and purple—that allow for a large variety of fabrics within each color.

Foundation paper is used for stability and to make it easier to achieve the correct-size block, but the blocks can be sewn without it. If you decide to use the paper foundation, a walking foot will help feed the paper and fabric evenly. Shorten your stitch length to make removing the foundation paper easier. Make sure that the paper is completely covered as you add the strips. Blocks need to be at least 16" (40.5 cm) square.

CUT YOUR FABRIC

WOF = width of fabric

Strips should vary from 1½" to 3½" (3.8 to 9 cm) wide and 8" to 24" (20.5 to 61 cm) long. Cut a variety of lengths, but be sure to have enough 24" (61 cm) long strips to fit diagonally across 24 blocks. If your scraps are shorter, cut extras so they can be pieced to make longer lengths.

From fabric A:

☐ Cut 120 strips.

From fabric B:

☐ Cut 100 strips.

From fabric C:

☐ Cut 48 squares in a variety of sizes from 2½" to 4½" (6.5 × 11.5 cm) for corner triangles.

From binding fabric:

☐ Cut 8 strips 2½" (6.5 cm) × WOF. Trim the selvedges.

From foundation paper:

☐ Cut 24 squares 16" × 16" (40.5 × 40.5 cm).

foundation paper

FIGURE 1

SEW THE BLOCKS

Note: Seam allowances are ¼" (6 mm).

① With right sides up, baste one fabric strip A diagonally across a paper foundation from corner to corner, sewing ⅛" (3 mm) from the raw edge (**figure 1**).

② With right sides facing, add a fabric strip B on top of the first strip A, matching long sides, then sew (**figure 2**). Open strip B and press.

③ Add another strip B to the opposite edge of strip A (**figure 3**).

④ Continue adding strips, alternating strips A and B until you approach the corner of the foundation paper.

⑤ Add a fabric C square corner triangle (page 7) to the outermost strips to cover the two corners (**figure 4**).

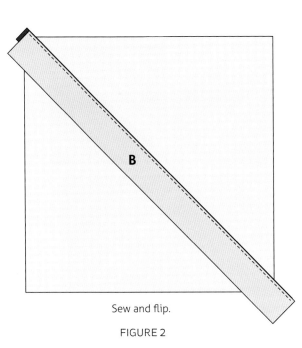

Sew and flip.

FIGURE 2

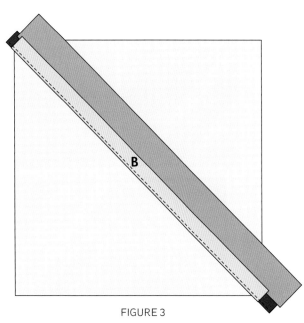

FIGURE 3

⑥ Following Steps 1–5, sew a total of twenty-four scrappy blocks. Remove the paper foundations.

⑦ Trim the blocks to 15½" × 15½" (39.5 × 39.5 cm).

ASSEMBLE THE TOP

⑧ You can orient the blocks in a variety of ways to create different effects. Here, the corner squares meet to create diamonds. Follow the Picnic Assembly Diagram on page 122 to assemble the blocks, choose an alternative from page 123, or design your own layout.

FINISH THE QUILT

⑨ Square the top, then pin it to the batting and backing fabric. Quilt as desired and add the binding. I quilted Picnic with simple horizontal straight lines. Turn to Tools and Techniques (page 6) for finishing techniques.

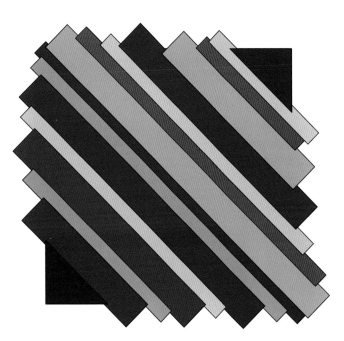

FIGURE 4

Picnic Assembly Diagram

VARIATIONS *on Picnic*

Simple changes in color placement can open up design possibilities. **The diagrams below show** two alternate ways to lay out your blocks.

In one Picnic variation, I made the purple corners bigger to emphasize the center strips. The blocks are also smaller, trimmed to only 6½" (16.5 cm) square. If you make fewer blocks than in the original design, this variation is a great simple gift when you are in a time crunch.

In the second variation, I oriented all of the stripes in the same direction. This creates additional, secondary stripes across the quilt top.

Or, try surrounding the blocks with expanses of more purple to further highlight the red and yellow stripes. This type of randomly pieced negative space is great for using smaller pieces of fabric. It adds interest and complexity without distracting from the focus.

If purple and orange are too deep for your recipient, this quilt would be sweet in pink and red piecing surrounded by a field of white or low-volume prints.

To quilt it, use echo stitching and straight-line stitching to emphasize different designs in your quilt. Complete the rest of the quilting with horizontal lines.

Picnic Alternate Layouts

GARDEN

FINISHED SIZE
70" × 86" (178 × 218 cm)

MATERIALS
- ☐ 2½ yd (2.3 m) total dark solid and print fabrics (A)
- ☐ 2½ yd (2.3 m) total light solid and print fabrics (B)
- ☐ ¾ yd (68.5 cm) solid yellow sashing fabric
- ☐ 5¼ yd (4.8 m) backing fabric
- ☐ ⅔ yd (61 cm) binding fabric
- ☐ 78" × 94" (198 × 239 cm) batting

TOOLS
- ☐ Basic Sewing Kit (page 6)

A simple, modern quilt often discards any sashing and borders. In Garden, the borders and sashing make up the entire quilt, becoming the blocks. Here, a mix of solids and prints that alternate dark and light create a whimsical story in a fun format.

The piano key rows are perfect for scraps, which also makes Garden a wonderful project to construct with a group. Instead of a block, assign each participant a row.

CUT YOUR FABRIC

WOF = width of fabric

From fabric A and B each:

☐ Cut 160 8½" (21.5 cm) strips that vary in width from 2" to 4½" (5 to 11.5 cm).

From sashing fabric:

☐ Cut 15 strips 1½" (3.8 cm) × WOF. Trim the selvedges.

> ▷ From 1 strip: Cut two 18½" (47 cm) lengths.

> ▷ From 2 strips: Cut two 32½" (82.5 cm) lengths.

> ▷ From 2 strips: Cut two 36½" (92.5 cm) lengths.

> Join the remaining WOF strips end to end as needed and cut the following lengths:

> ▷ Two 50½" (128.5 cm) strips

> ▷ Two 54½" (138.5 cm) strips

> ▷ Two 68½" (174 cm) strips

From binding fabric:

☐ Cut 8 strips 2½" (6.5 cm) × WOF. Trim the selvedges.

Tip: The narrow sashing strips are easy to stretch and distort. Be sure to handle them carefully.

SEW THE ROWS

Note: All seam allowances are ¼" (6 mm).

① Make the rows by alternating light and dark strips. With right sides facing, sew the 8½" (21.5 cm) long edges together **(figure 1)**.

② Continue sewing the strips to make sixteen rows in the following lengths, trimming strips as needed **(figure 2)**:

☐ Four 16½" (42 cm) strips

☐ Four 34½" (87.5 cm) strips

☐ Four 52½" (133.5 cm) strips

☐ Four 70½" (179 cm) strips

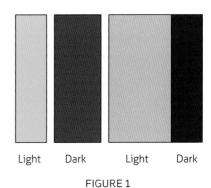

Light   Dark   Light   Dark

FIGURE 1

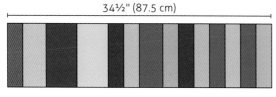

16½" (42 cm)

Make 4.

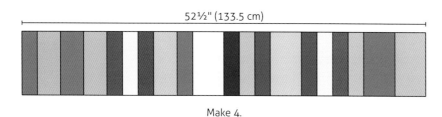

34½" (87.5 cm)

Make 4.

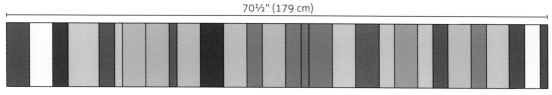

52½" (133.5 cm)

Make 4.

70½" (179 cm)

Make 4.

FIGURE 2

ASSEMBLE THE TOP

③ Assemble the top according to the Garden Assembly Diagram on page 128. Starting in the center of the quilt and with right sides facing, sew two 8½" × 16½" (21.5 × 42 cm) rows together to form a square with a vertical seam. Add the remaining two 8½" × 16½" (21.5 × 42 cm) rows, sewing one on the upper edge of the square and one on the lower edge of the square to form a rectangle.

④ With right sides facing, add a 1½" × 32½" (3.8 × 82.5 cm) sashing strip to each side of the rectangle. Add the 1½" × 18½" (3.8 × 47 cm) sashing strips to the top and bottom.

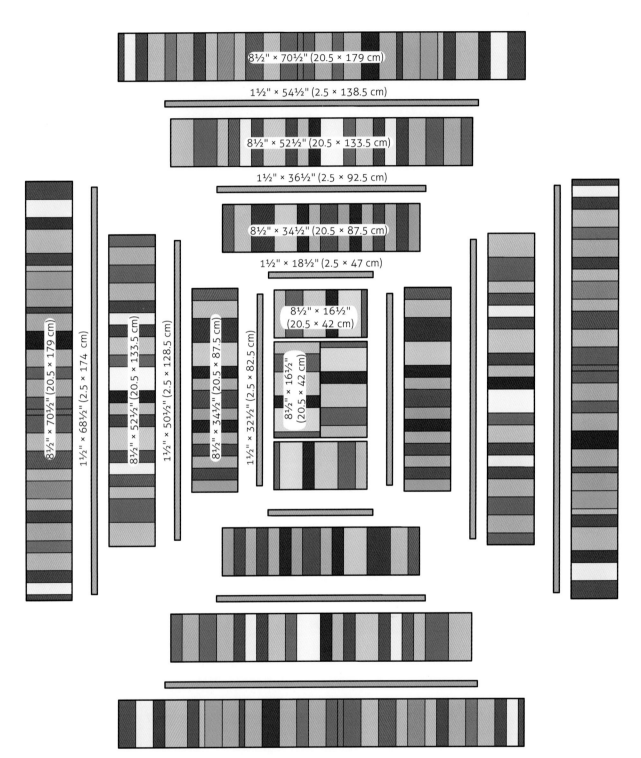

Garden Assembly Diagram

⑤ With right sides facing, add one 8½" × 34½" (21.5 × 87.5 cm) row to each side of the pieced rectangle. Sew the remaining 8½" × 34½" (21.5 × 87.5 cm) rows to the top and bottom.

⑥ With right sides facing, sew a 1½" × 50½" (3.8 × 128.5 cm) sashing strip to each side of the pieced rectangle. Then add the 1½" × 36½" (3.8 × 92.5 cm) sashing strips to the top and bottom.

⑦ With right sides facing, sew one 8½" × 52½" (21.5 × 133.5 cm) row to either side of the top. Then add the remaining 8½" × 52½" (21.5 × 133.5 cm) rows to the top and bottom.

⑧ With right sides facing, sew a 1½" × 68½" (3.8 × 174 cm) sashing strip to each side of the rectangle. Then sew the 1½" × 54½" (3.8 × 138.5 cm) sashing strips to the top and bottom.

⑨ With right sides facing, add one 8½" × 70½" (21.5 × 179 cm) row to each side of the rectangle. Sew the remaining 8½" × 70½" (21.5 × 179 cm) rows to the top and bottom.

FINISH THE QUILT

⑩ Square the top, then pin it to the backing and the batting. Quilt as desired, then add the binding. I quilted Garden in an allover graphic square pattern. Turn to Tools and Techniques (page 6) for finishing techniques.

NEST

FINISHED SIZE
61½" × 82" (156 × 208 cm)

MATERIALS
- ☐ ¼ yd (23 cm) total solid and print red fabrics (A)
- ☐ 3 yd (2.75 m) total solid and print blue, green, and chartreuse fabrics (B)
- ☐ 4 yd (3.7 m) total solid and print aqua sashing fabrics (C)
- ☐ 5 yd (4.6 m) backing fabric
- ☐ ⅔ yd (61 cm) binding fabric
- ☐ 70" × 90" (178 × 229 cm) batting

TOOLS
- ☐ Basic Sewing Kit (page 6)

Improvisational piecing is an effective technique for creating a group quilt, especially if the participants vary in their sewing abilities. You can choose the fabrics and overall color theme, but they get to make individual decisions about which fabric to put where. The crazy log cabin block gives them a structure to follow, while allowing creative freedom within the block. You will be amazed how beautifully it will all come together. The fun of the crazy log cabin block is that you can always add more strips or trim off extra fabric.

This type of quilt is very forgiving and perfect for collaborating. The blocks in my Nest were all sewn by differently abled adults, and then more Bright Hopes volunteers added the turquoise sashing to reach the final block size. For Nest, we started with the traditional red center of a log cabin quilt. To highlight the red, we surrounded it with a group of analogous colors—greens and blues for the logs and turquoise sashing.

CUT YOUR FABRIC

From fabric A:

☐ Cut 12 squares and rectangles in a variety of sizes from 2½" to 4½" (6.5 to 11.5 cm).

From fabric B:

☐ Cut several strips that are 1½" to 4" (3.8 to 10 cm) wide and 4" to 15" (10 to 38 cm) long.

From fabric C:

☐ Cut the sashing strips to fit the finished blocks.

From binding fabric:

☐ Cut 8 strips 2½" (6.5 cm) × WOF. Trim the selvedges.

SEW THE BLOCKS

Note: All seam allowances are ¼ " (6 mm).

① Start with a fabric A square or rectangle in the center. Choose a fabric B strip that is at least as long as one side of the center piece. With right sides facing, sew fabric B to one side of the center piece.

Open the fabric and press the seam. Trim any of the fabric B strip that extends beyond the center piece.

② Continue to add fabric B strips around the center piece, trimming as necessary **(figure 1)**. If the strips are not long enough, piece two or more together, stitching the short ends, right sides facing.

Stop adding strips when the block is 10" to 15" (25.5 cm to 38 cm) square.

③ Following Steps 1 and 2, sew twelve blocks in a variety of sizes from 10" to 15" (25.5 cm to 38 cm) square.

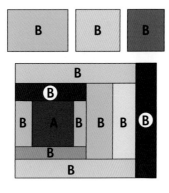

FIGURE 1

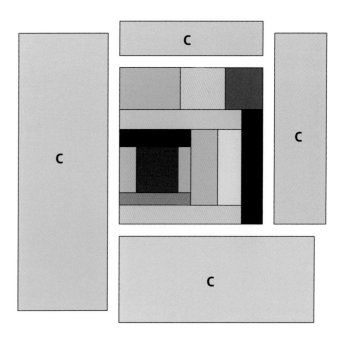

FIGURE 2

ASSEMBLE THE TOP

④ Add the sashing to make each block at least 21" (53.5 cm) square. For most of the blocks in this quilt, I used four strips of sashing, although there are a few blocks that have extra sashing strips.

Cut fabric C into 5" to 7" (12.5 to 18 cm) wide strips from 10" to 22" (25.5 to 56 cm) long. The length and the width of the strips will depend on the size of the block.

⑤ Choose a piece of fabric C sashing at least as long as one side of the block. With right sides facing, sew the fabric C strip to the block.

Open the fabric and press the seam. Trim any of the fabric C strip that extends beyond the block.

⑥ Continue to add fabric C strips around the block, trimming as necessary, until the block is at least 21" (53.5 cm) square **(figure 2)**. Trim to 21" (53.5 cm), noting that the pieced portion will not necessarily be centered.

⑦ Follow the Nest Assembly Diagram on page 135 to create a grid with three rows across and four rows down.

Because your blocks will be different than mine, lay them out before sewing together. You may want to swap or turn some blocks so that your colors and light and dark areas are balanced.

FINISH THE QUILT

⑧ Square the top, then pin it to the backing and batting. Quilt as desired, then add the binding. I quilted Nest simply with randomly spaced horizontal lines. Turn to Tools and Techniques (page 6) for finishing techniques.

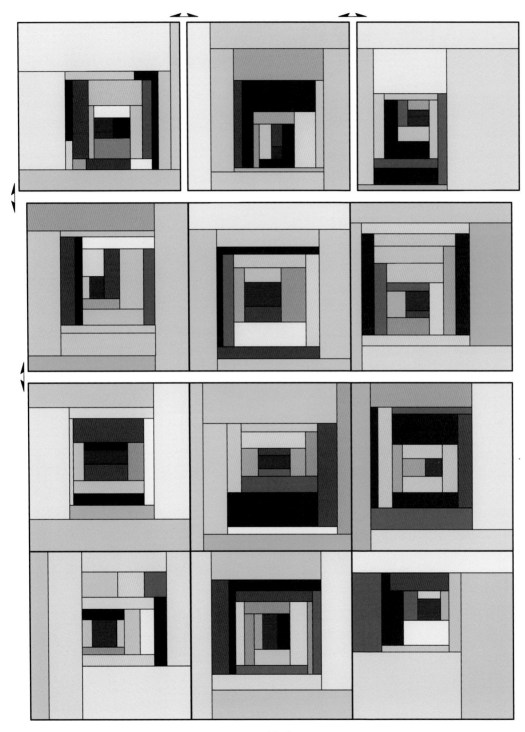

Nest Assembly Diagram

VARIATION *on Nest*

With so many wonderful artists and illustrators designing fabric, making an I-Spy quilt is more fun than ever. The improvisational piecing in Nest just adds to the fun. Instead of the red centers for this variation of Nest, I fussy-cut specific images from fabric for the centers. When lining up your ruler to fussy-cut images, make sure to add a ¼" (6 mm) seam allowance all the way around.

I chose twenty-five different images from some of my favorite fabrics. To highlight these special elements, each image is surrounded by low-volume prints and a variety of solid whites and off-whites, including flannel and linen to add texture.

Trim the twenty-five blocks to 8½" (21.5 cm) square and assemble them into a simple 5 × 5 grid. Now what? Make the quilt more dynamic by scooting that unit of blocks over to the side. Surround it on three sides with bold solids in tints and shades of red to pick up some of the colors in the images.

I quilted the I-Spy blocks in random connected squares and rectangles and the background in random vertical lines.

Templates

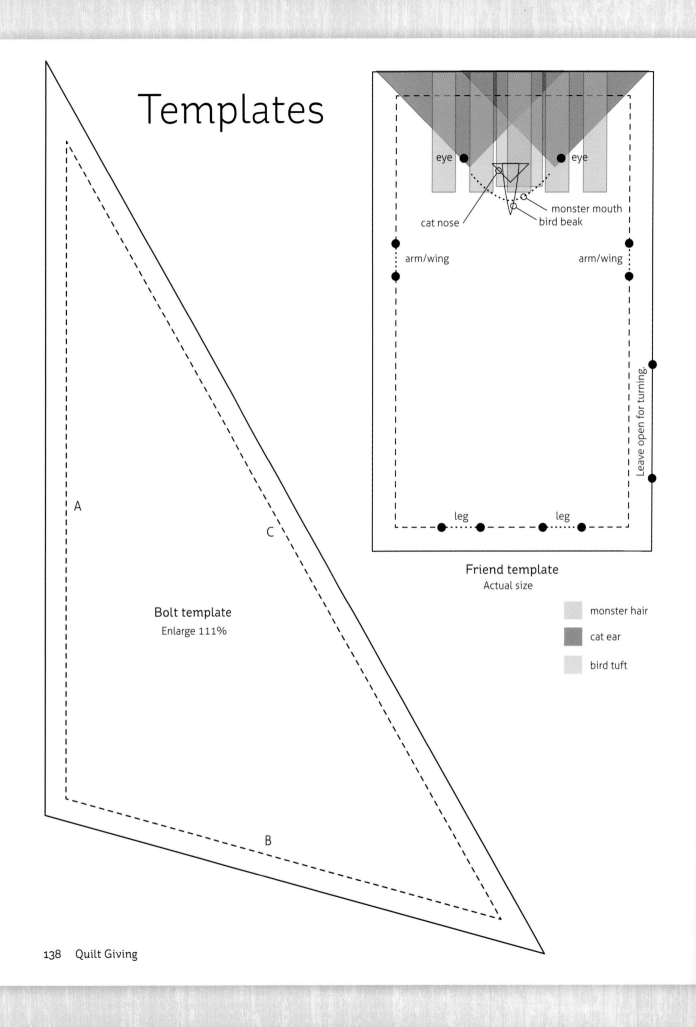

Bolt template
Enlarge 111%

A

B

C

Friend template
Actual size

eye · eye

cat nose
bird beak
monster mouth

arm/wing · arm/wing

Leave open for turning.

leg · leg

monster hair
cat ear
bird tuft

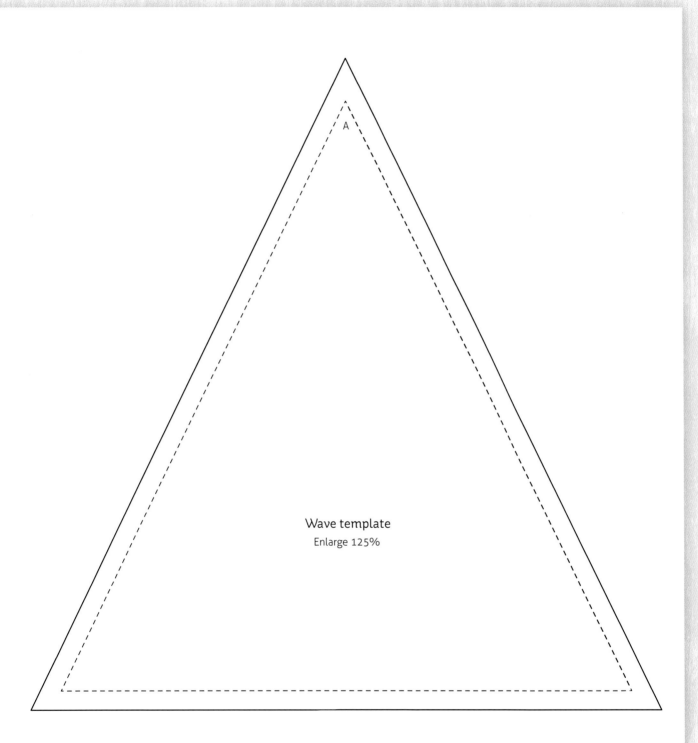

A

Wave template

Enlarge 125%

Resources

Many of the materials for the projects in this book were very generously supplied by:

ART GALLERY FABRICS
artgalleryfabrics.com

AURIFIL
aurifil.com

CLOUD9 FABRICS
cloud9fabrics.com

IN THE BEGINNING FABRICS
inthebeginningfabrics.com

MICHAEL MILLER FABRICS
michaelmillerfabrics.com

ROBERT KAUFMAN FABRICS
robertkaufman.com

Any materials remaining from the project samples in this book will be donated to the Bright Hopes Collaborative Quilt Project quilts and programs as well as other not-for-profit programs.

Online Resources

HAWTHORNE THREADS
hawthornethreads.com

MARMALADE FABRICS
marmaladefabrics.com

PINK CASTLE FABRICS
pinkcastlefabrics.com

PURL SOHO
purlsoho.com

QUILTBUG QUILT SHOP (BATTING)
quiltbug.com

SPOONFLOWER (FABRIC AND LABELS)
spoonflower.com

About the Author

Deborah Fisher is an object maker, idea generator, designer of sewn things, and the author of *Sew Fun: 20 Projects for the Whole Family.* She is the director of two nonprofit organizations, the Bright Hopes Collaborative Quilt Project in New York and Bo Twal, an international doll project. She is very fond of her two daughters, her husband, Mordy the marmalade cat, and cocoa. Find out more about her projects at fishmuseumandcircus.com and @fishmuseum on Instagram.

Index

Editor LESLIE T. O'NEILL

Technical Editor LINDA TURNER
GRIEPENTROG

Photography DONALD SCOTT

Cover and interior design
KERRY JACKSON

Illustrations MISSY SHEPLER

_fw_

www.fwcommunity.com

19 18 17 16 15   5 4 3 2 1

Distributed in Canada by Fraser Direct
100 Armstrong Avenue
Georgetown, ON, Canada L7G 5S4
Tel: (905) 877-4411

Distributed in the U.K. and Europe by
F&W MEDIA INTERNATIONAL
Brunel House, Newton Abbot,
Devon, TQ12 4PU, England
Tel: (+44) 1626 323200
Fax: (+44) 1626 323319
E-mail: enquiries@fwmedia.com

Distributed in Australia by Capricorn Link
P.O. Box 704, S. Windsor NSW,
2756 Australia
Tel: (02) 4560 1600, Fax: (02) 4577 5288
E-mail: books@capricornlink.com.au

SRN 15QM04
ISBN 978-1-62033-885-8 (pbk.)
ISBN 978-1-62033-886-5 (PDF)

Dedication

To Andy, who built us a home of peace,
and to my Dad, who helped him.

With very special thanks to all of the
women of the Bright Hopes Collaborative
Quilt Project whose generosity of time
and spirit fills my soul. These women are
mighty. They are friends, sisters, aunts,
mothers, and grandmothers, loyal and
fierce. Thank you for sharing the journey
and for hanging on through this wild and
bumpy ride.

Acknowledgments

With thanks and wishes for a cozy quilt and a big cup of cocoa:

To my beautiful Mom, for the sunshine that made the seed grow.

To Aunt Joanie, for providing the initial seed.

To Hazelnut and Bippy, for their squooshy, fill-up-my-heart hugs.

My deepest gratitude to Léonie Davis and her welcoming committee for opening up her studio to me.

Thanks to Leslie O'Neill, Kerry Bogert, and everyone at Interweave for navigating through stormy skies to reach a clear day.

To everyone who has been a part of Bright Hopes through the years, including the kids at the Little Flower Children's Residence, the adults at the Day Services East treatment program, the scout troops, the youth groups, and all the rest, thank you for joining us on this adventure. And to all the Bright Hopes supporters, from raffle-ticket buyers to annual appeal supporters to yard-sale donators, thank you, thank you, and thank you!

And of course to my Mordy for his sweet company. Thanks for holding down the fabric.

Circus blocks were created by these members of Stash Bee-2014 Hive 9: Jennifer Barclay, Beky Branagan, Shelby Faux, Lynn Hurst, Renae Micchea, Karen Morrison, and Elita Sharpe.

Nest blocks were created by the following people from Family Residences and Essential Enterprises, Inc.'s Day Service program, located in East Setauket, New York, under the supervision of Carole Smith: Antoinette A., Courtney L., Diana V., Thomas R., and Wanda B., with additional piecing by Joyce Bonitch, Laurie Friedman, and Lynn Kamen of the Bright Hopes Collaborative Quilt Project.

Picnic and Garden blocks were created by these members of the Bright Hopes Collaborative Quilt Project: Joyce Bonitch, Ronni Camhi, Joan Cash, Joan David, Lois Davila, Léonie Davis, Kelly Doerge, Helen Emmerich, Eileen Fisher, Laurie Friedman, Joan Korins, Janet Montelione, Barbara Siegel, Barbara Staab, Clione Stancik, and Corinne Wilson.

Fabric collages were created by these members of the Sea Rockets 4-H Club of Suffolk County in New York: Dasi Cash, Hazel Cash, Patrick Heintzelman, Aviv Nieroda, Tahvo Nieroda, Finn Reynolds, Genevieve Reynolds, Penelope Reynolds, Jaden Rosado, and Jake Rosado.

City, Bolt, and Twinkle were quilted by Emme Nichols of brownhousestudiosquilting.com.

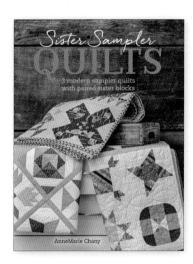